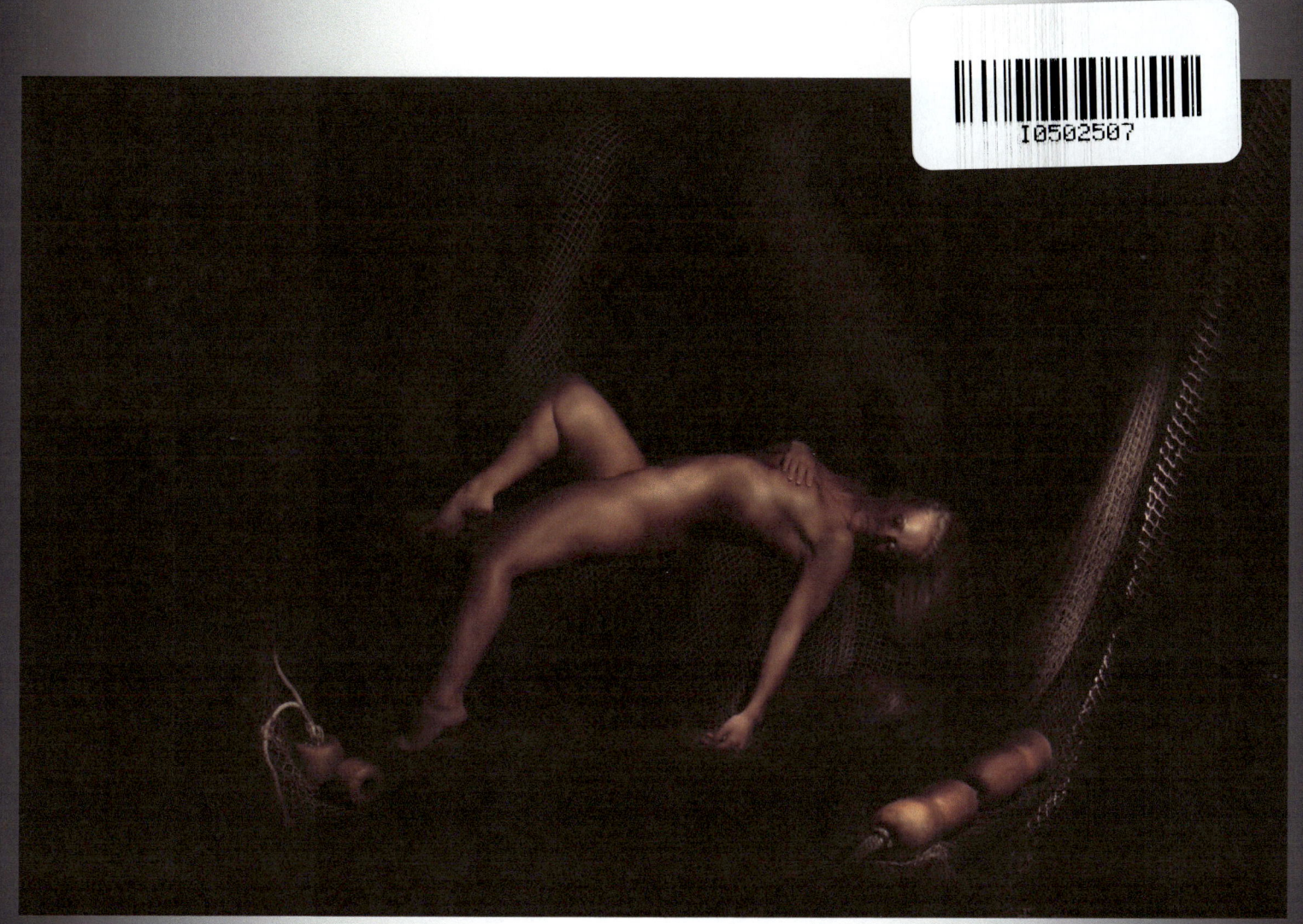

Tavart Nudes in this the second volume will show what we have done with a very dark scene and a flashlight. Human form is always such a beautiful thing and can be captured in so many ways. Long exposures low lights seem always to make art nudes so much better. Each image could be shot time and time again with a deferent look each time. The reason being you are painting the image with a flashlight and to repeat each image the same can not be done. A love affair with light painting models is something that happens each time you see the images. Trying to paint on canvas with paints has never been something I could do, But this makes me feel as though I can paint. Please enjoy our images in this and all our art books. My Best Robert Tavernier

© 2013 Robert Tavernier

1

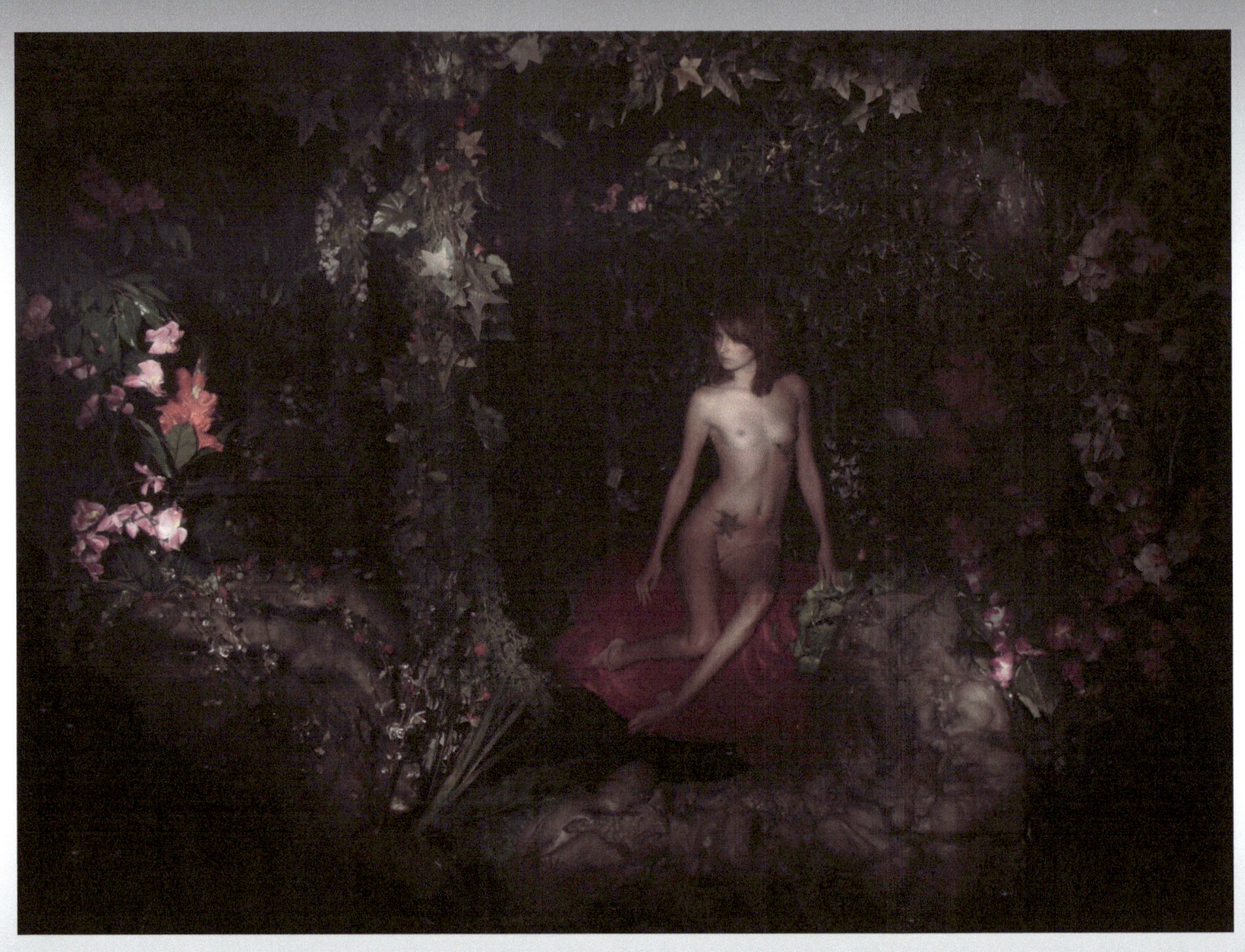

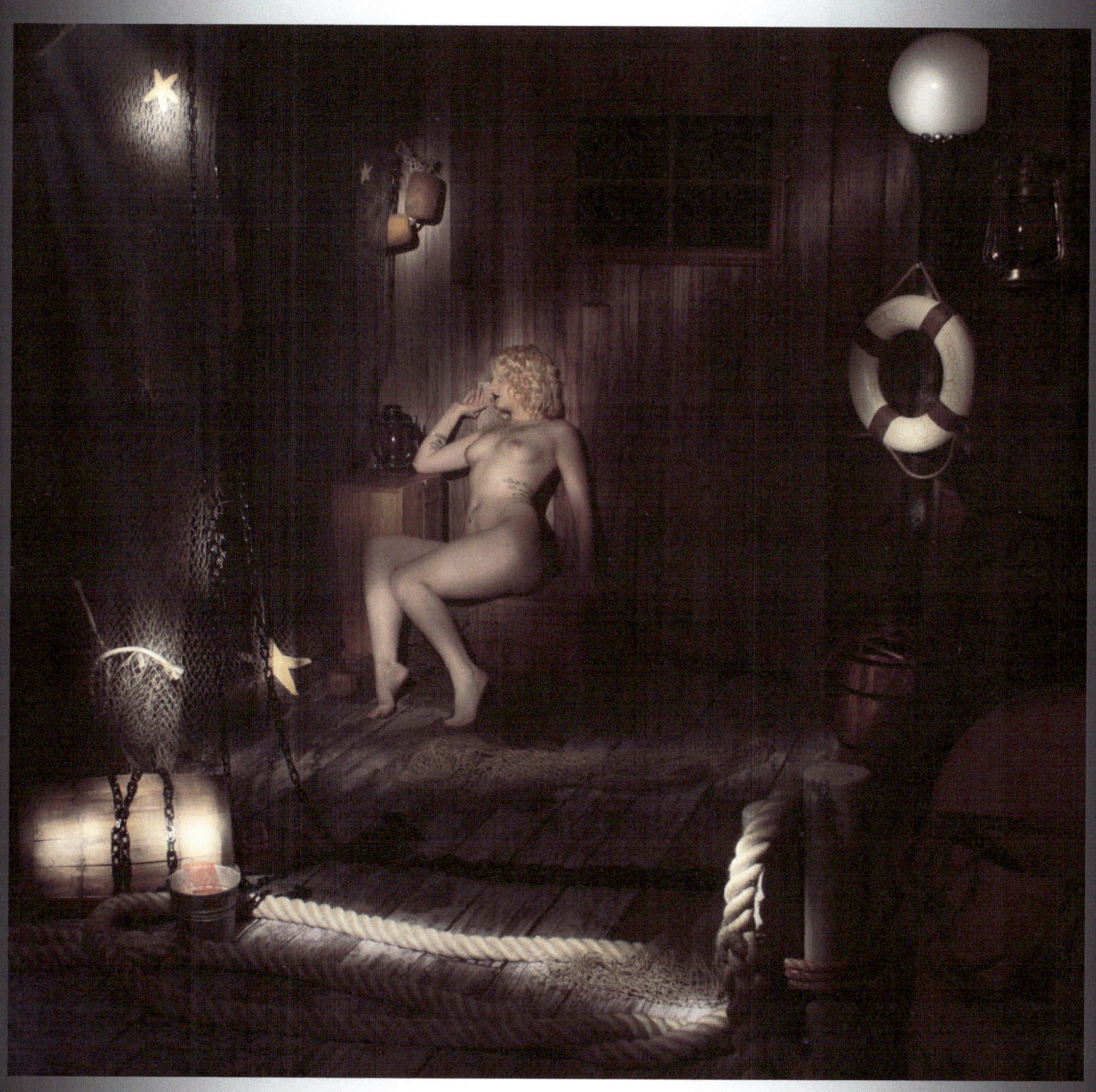

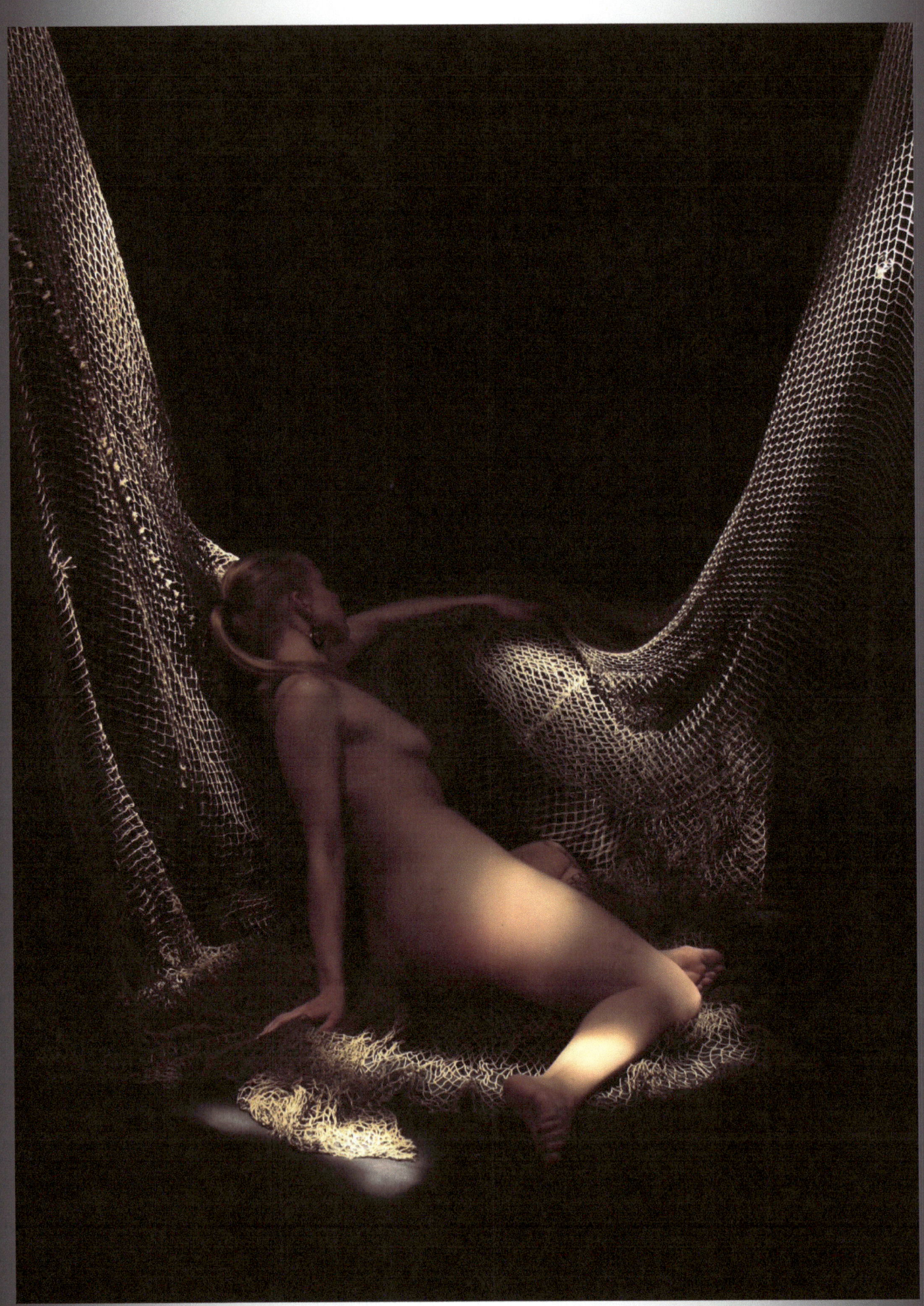

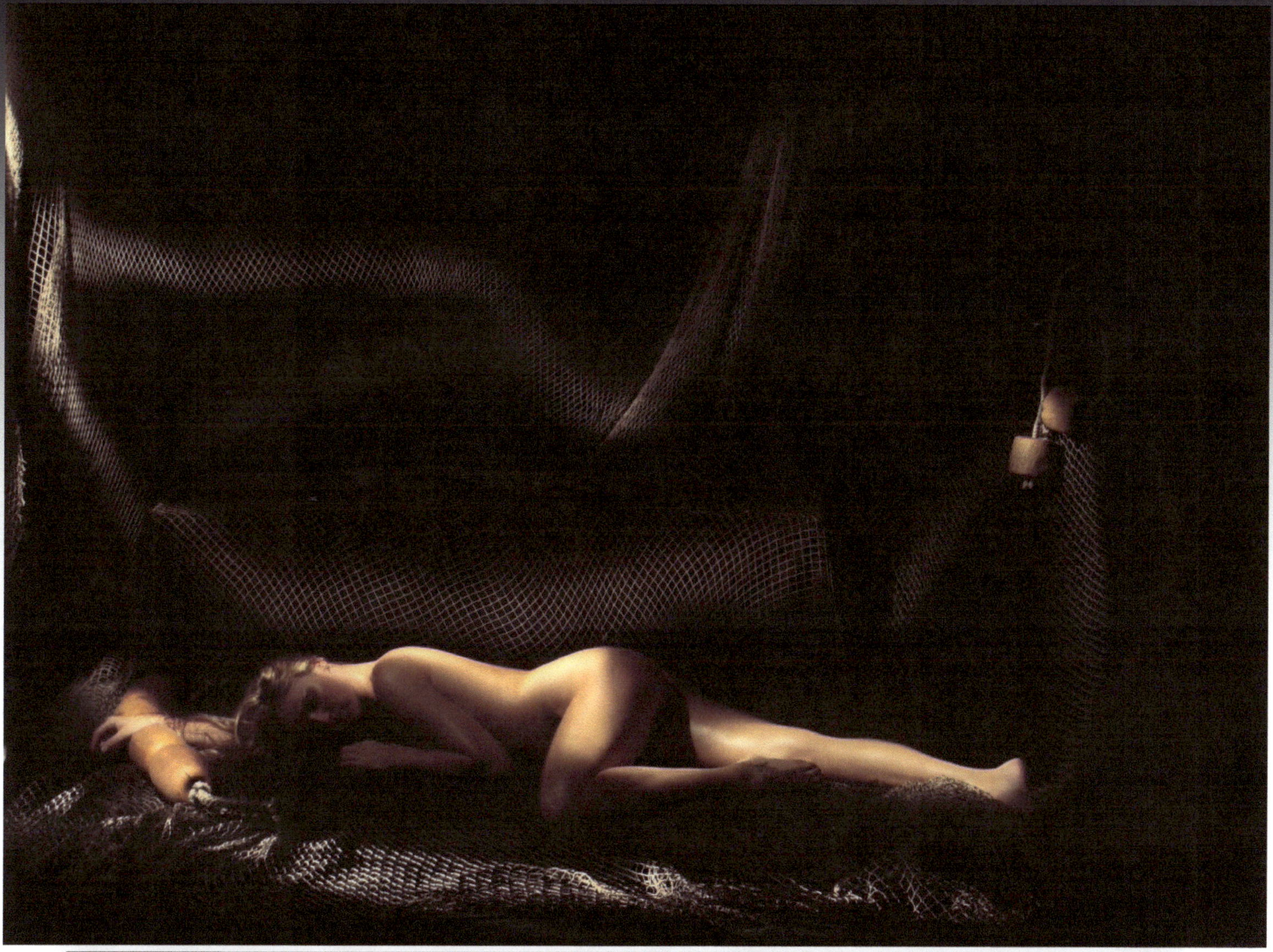

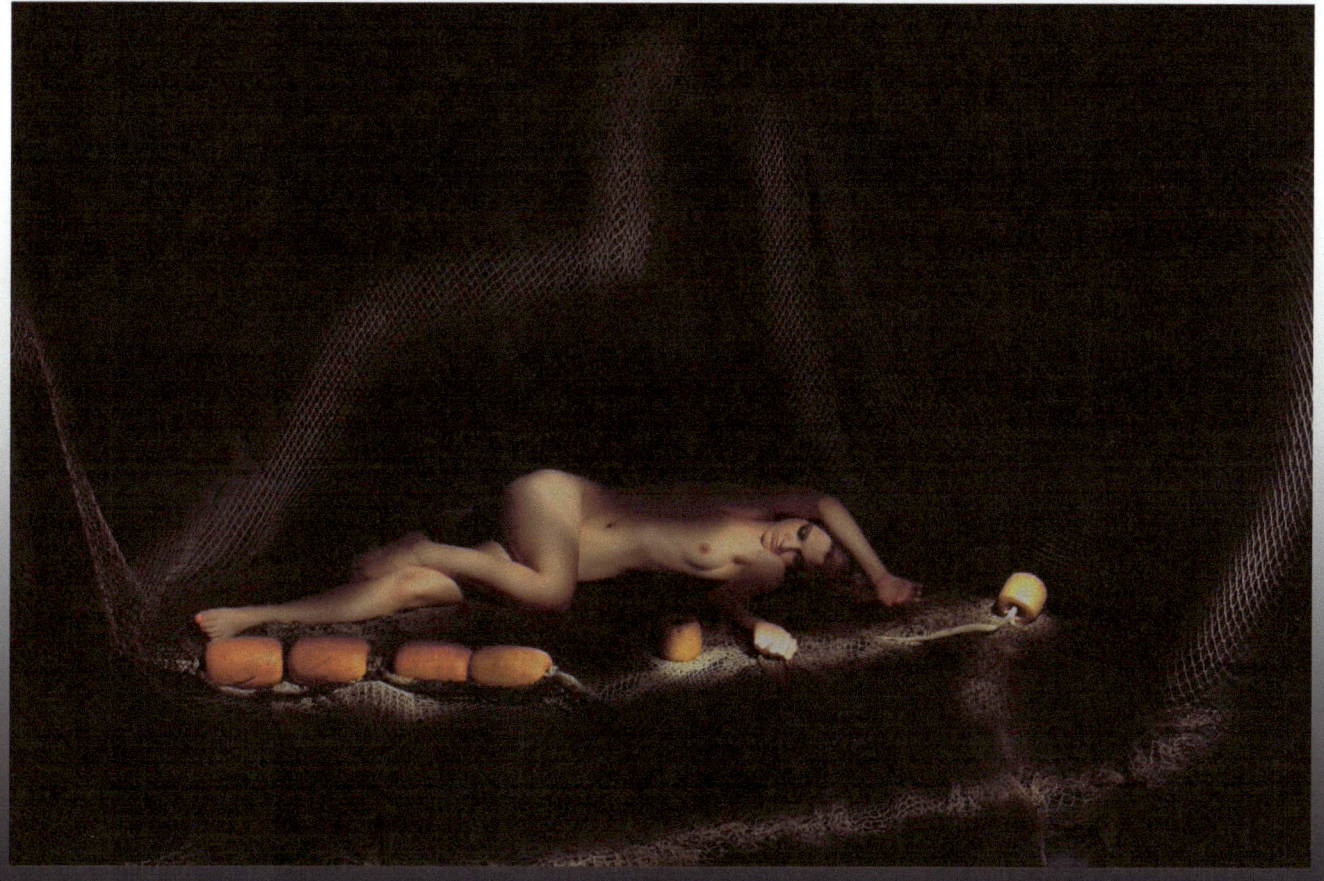

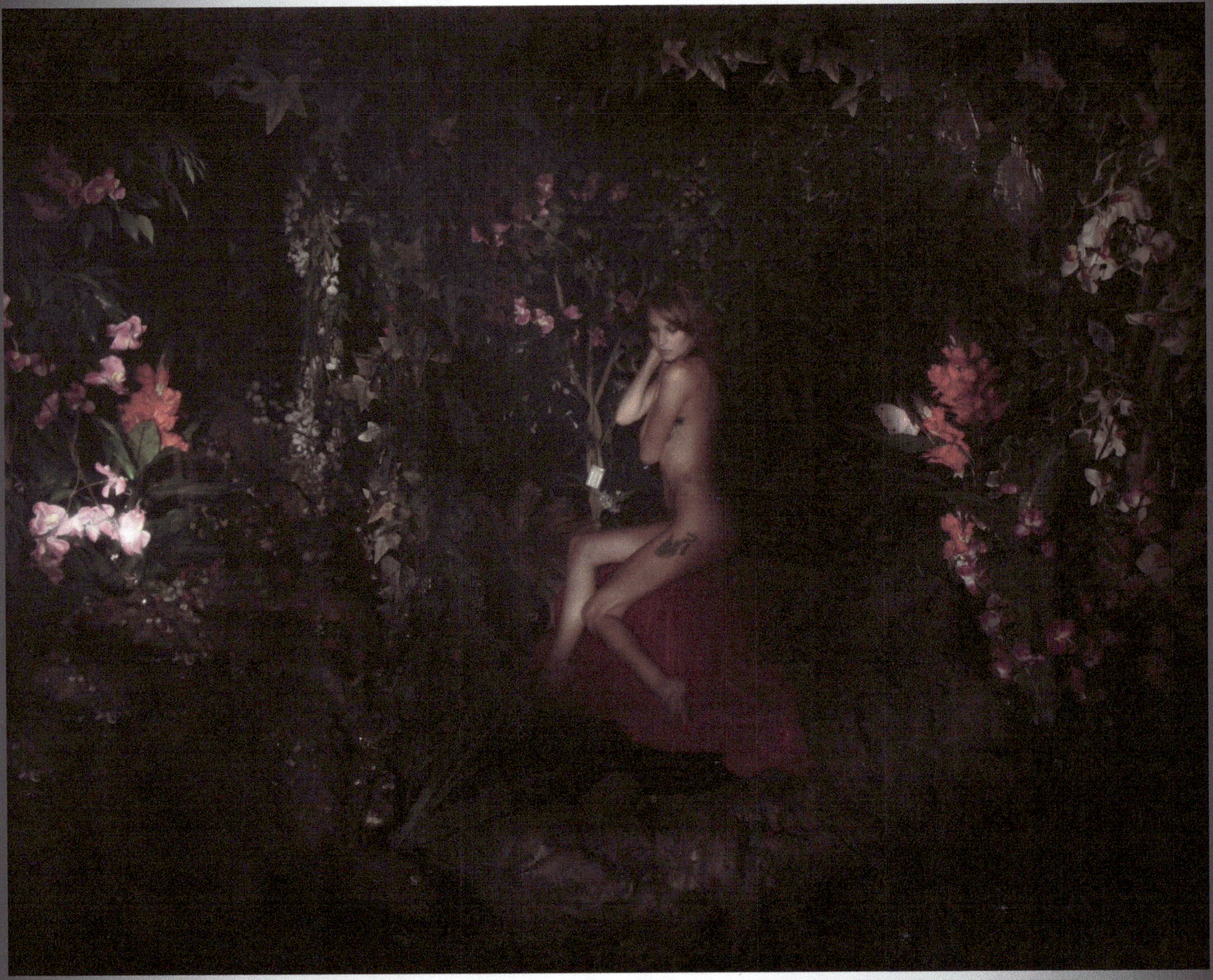

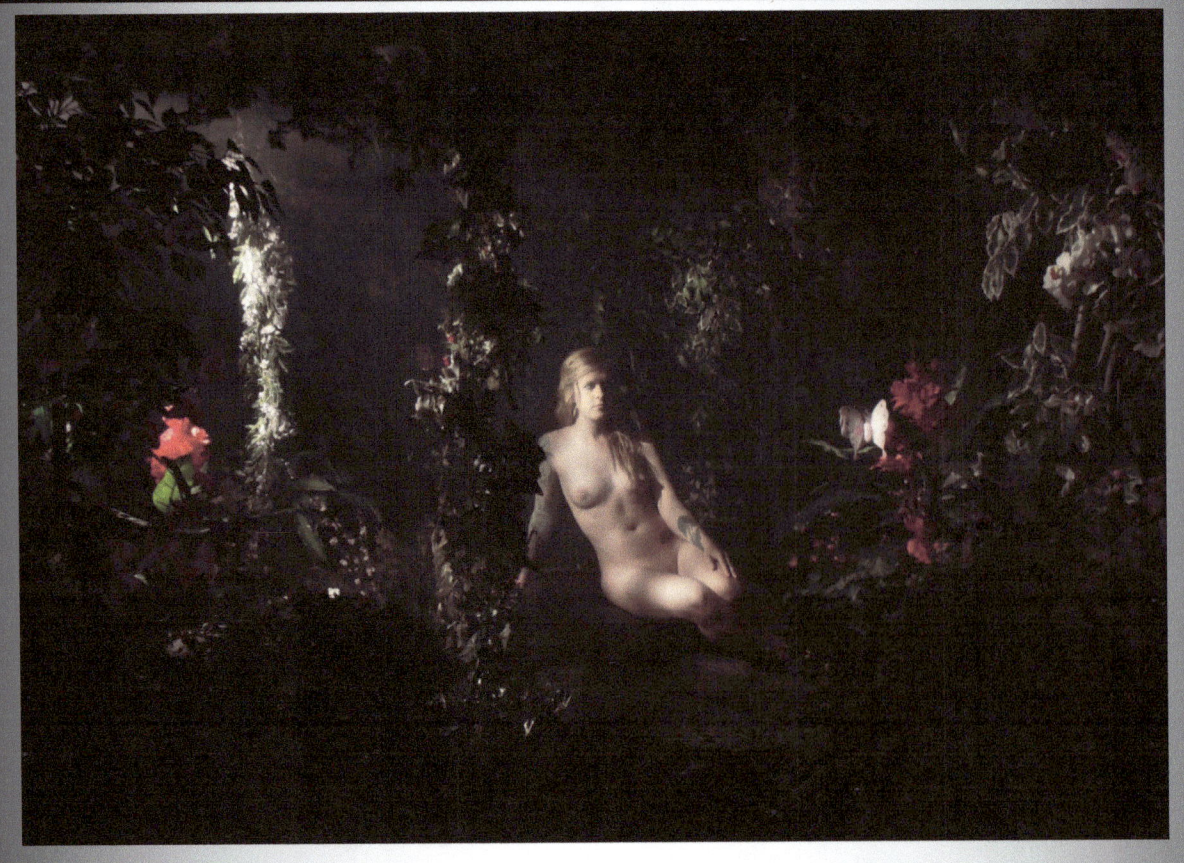

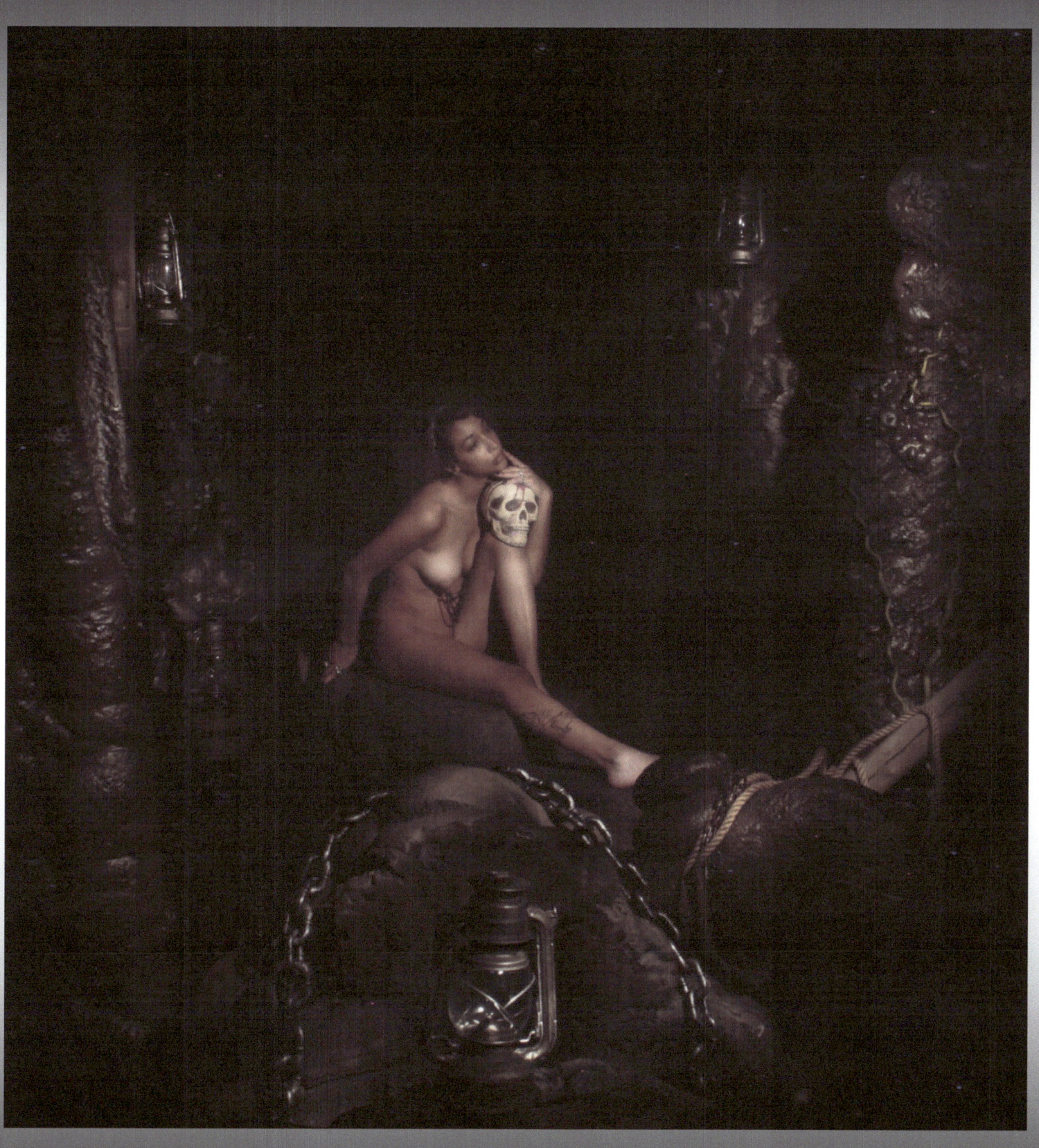

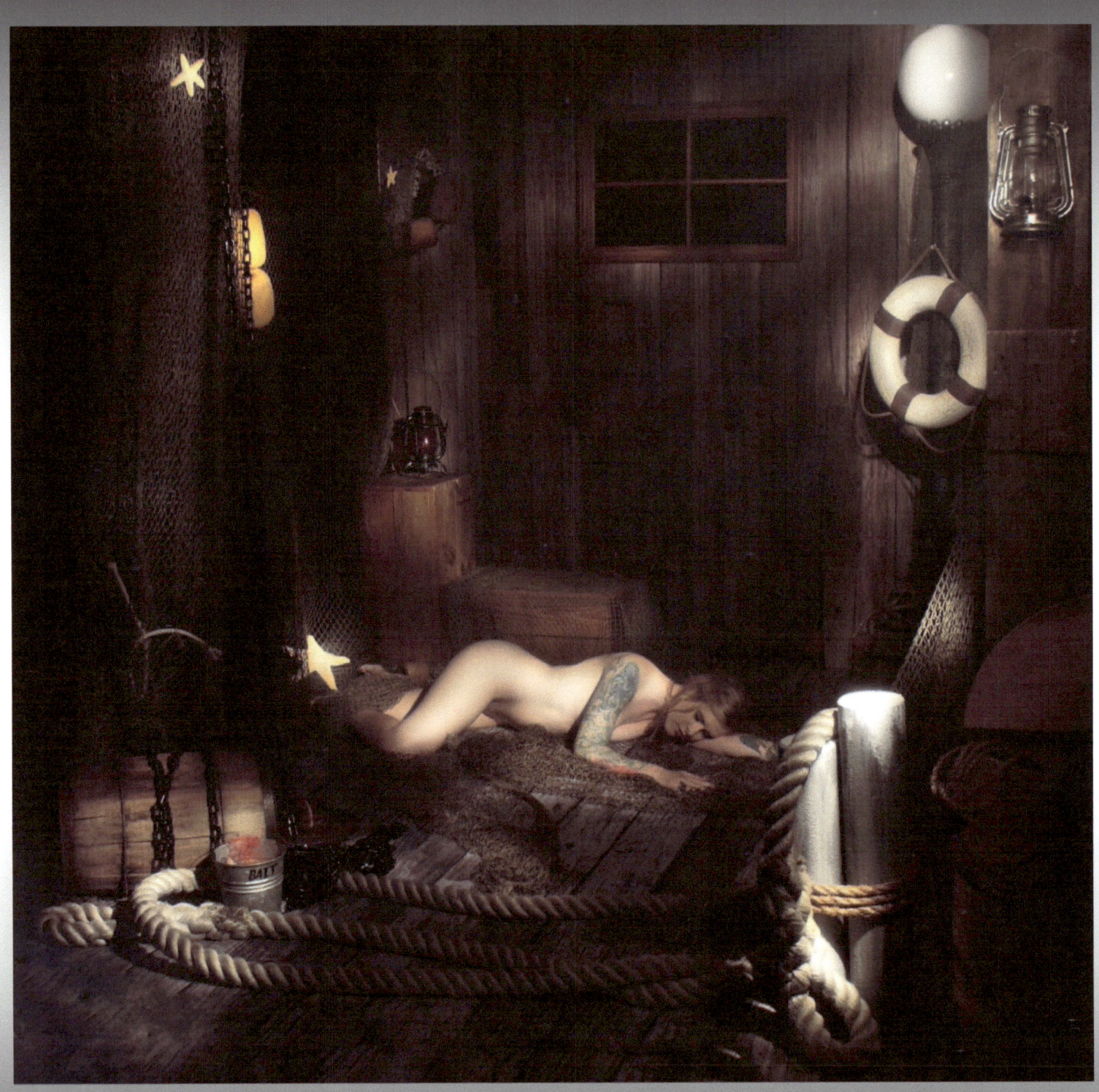

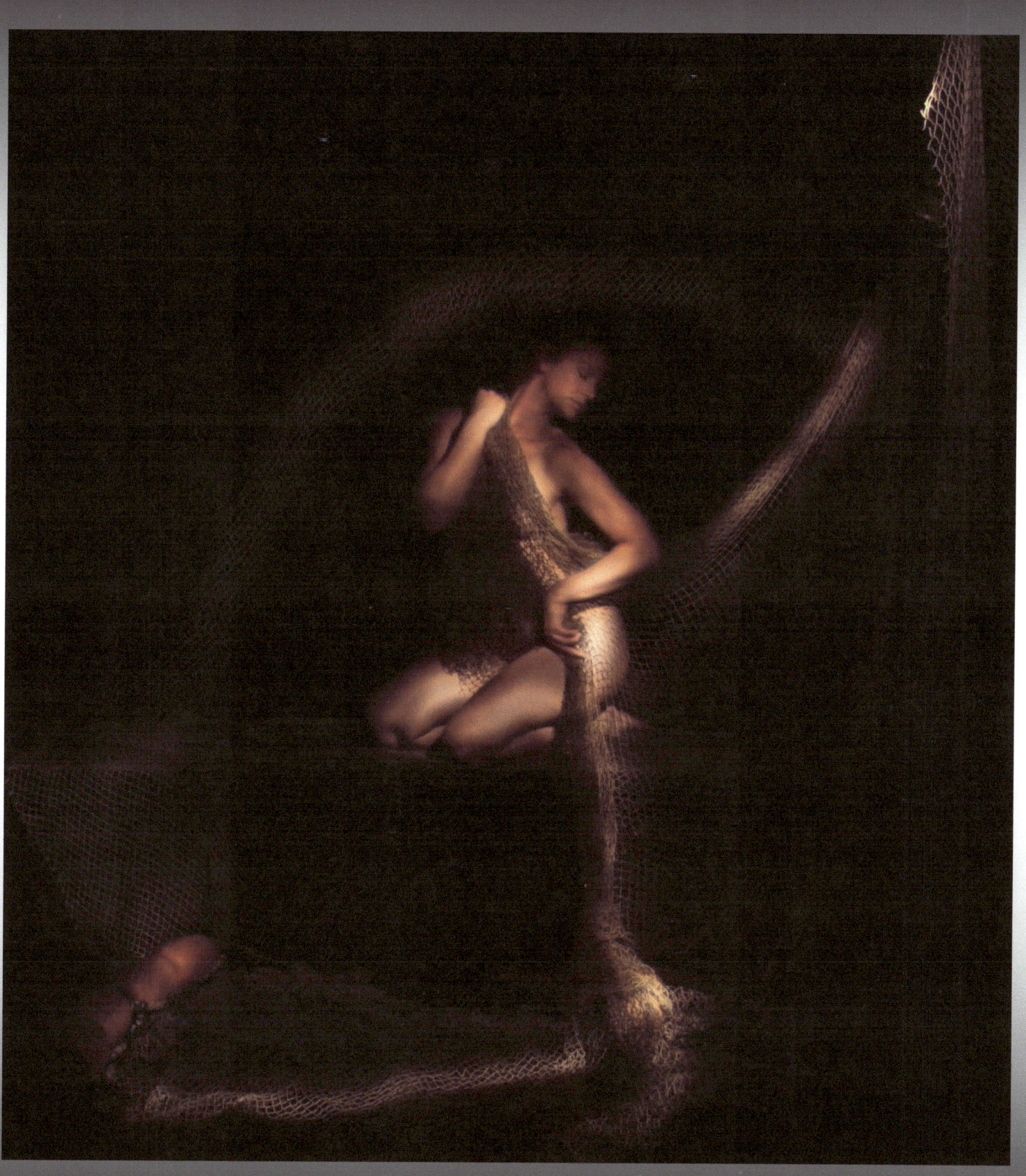

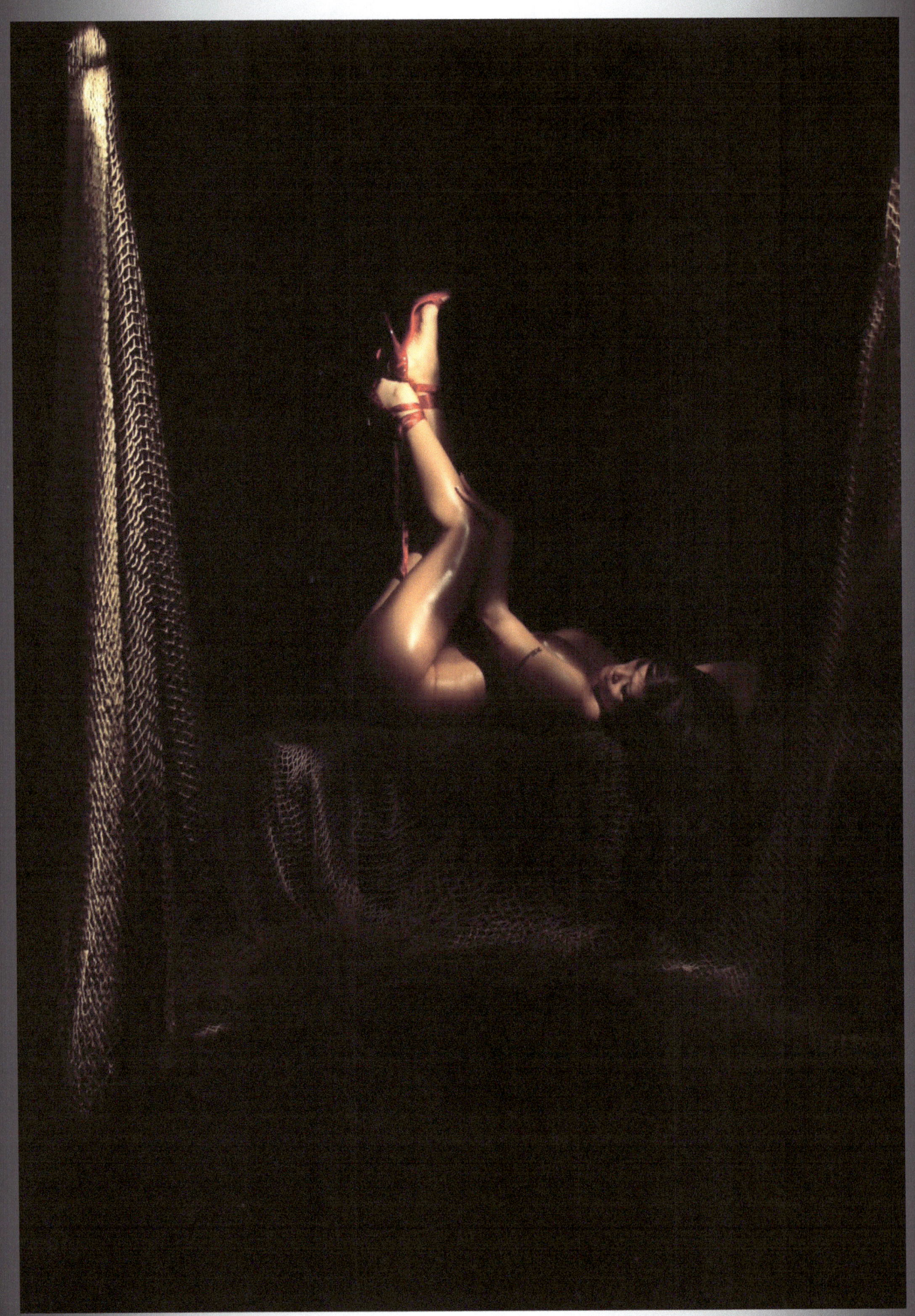

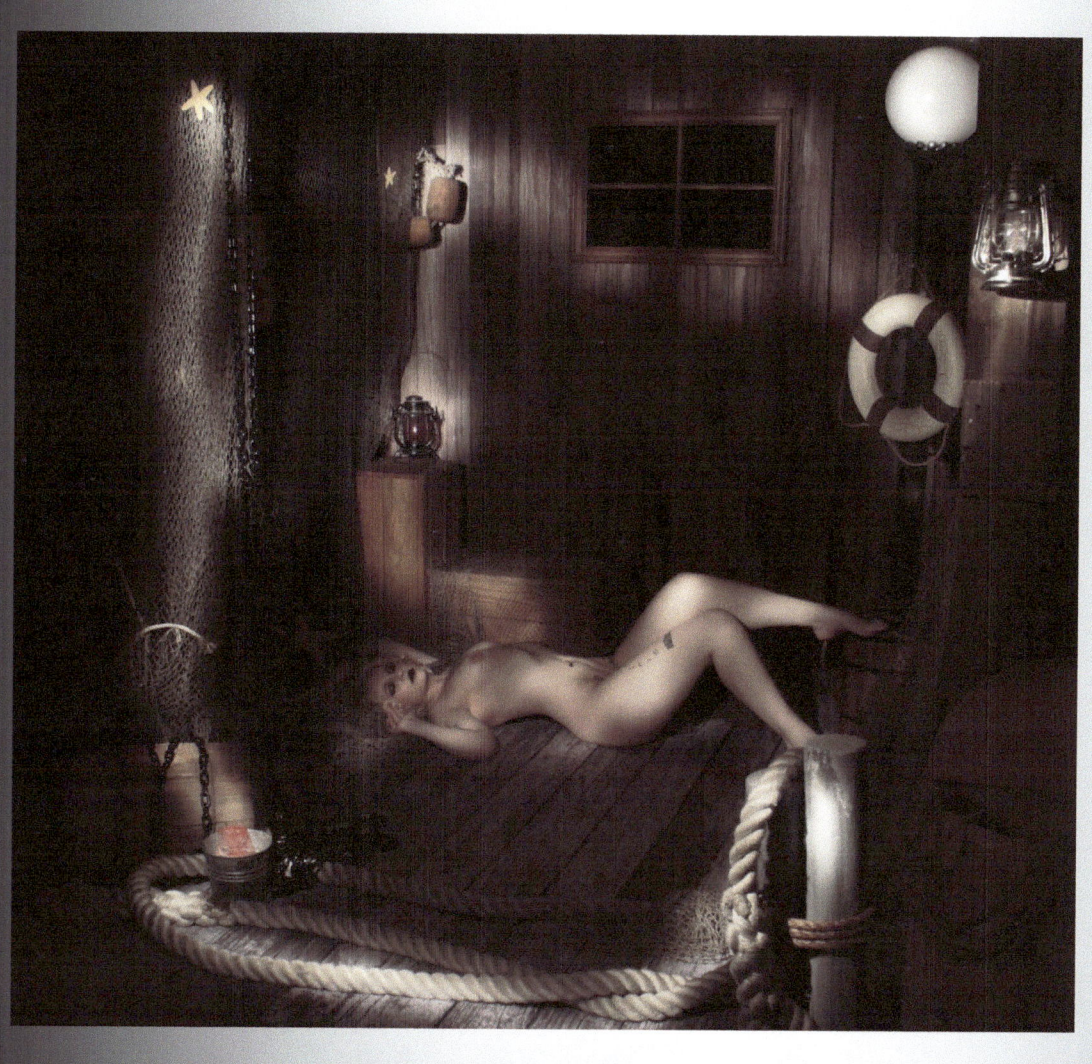

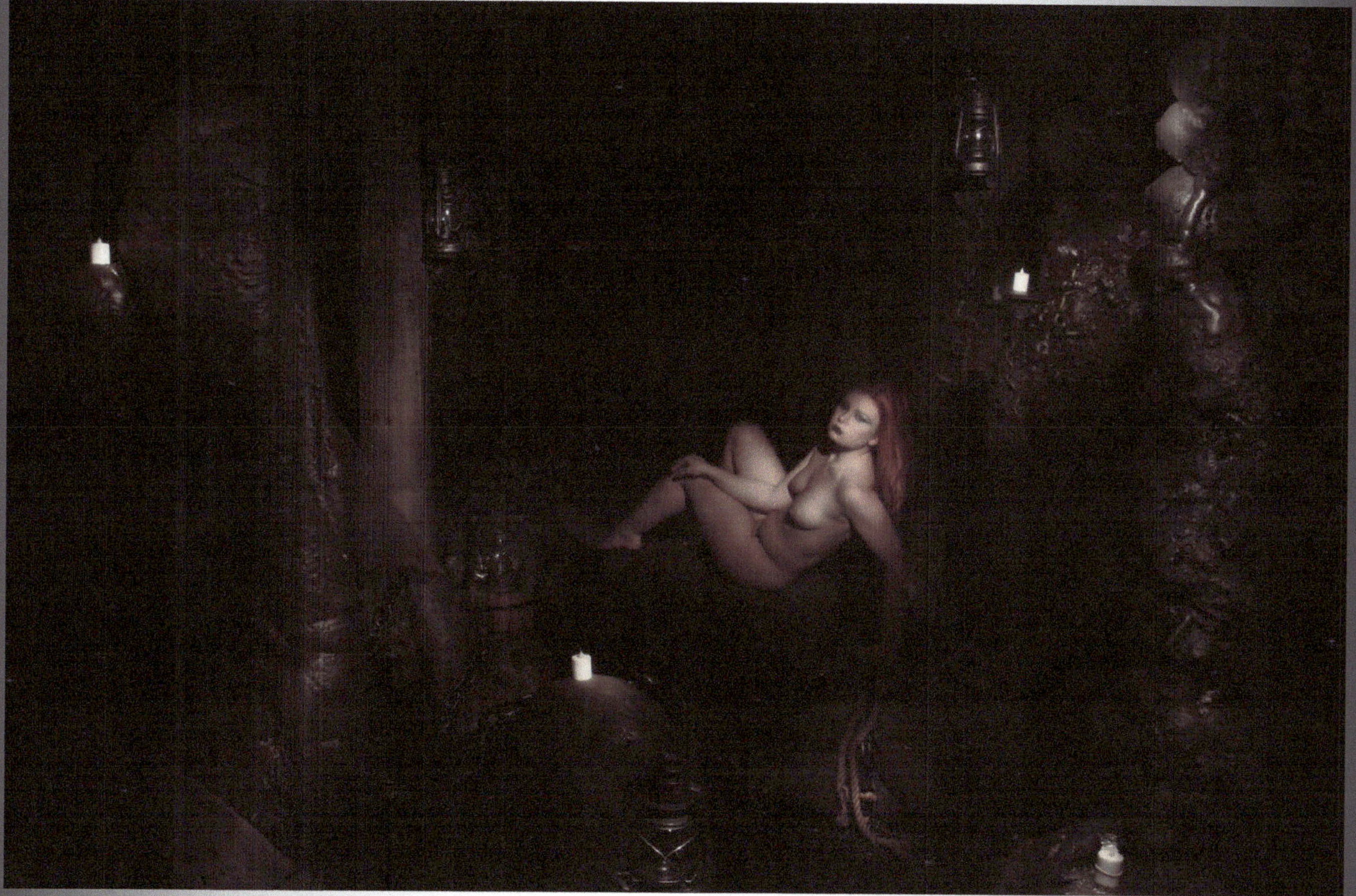

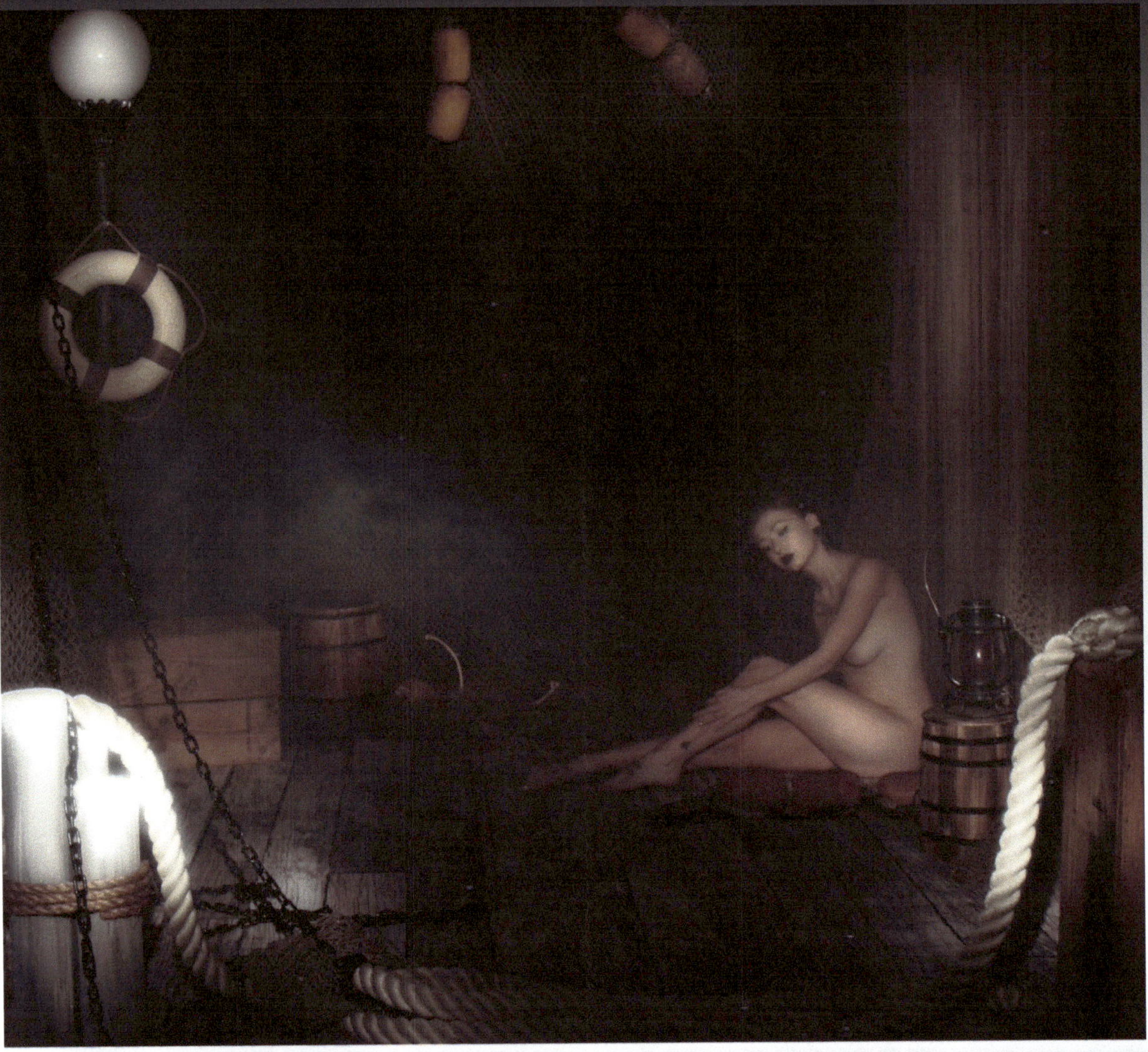

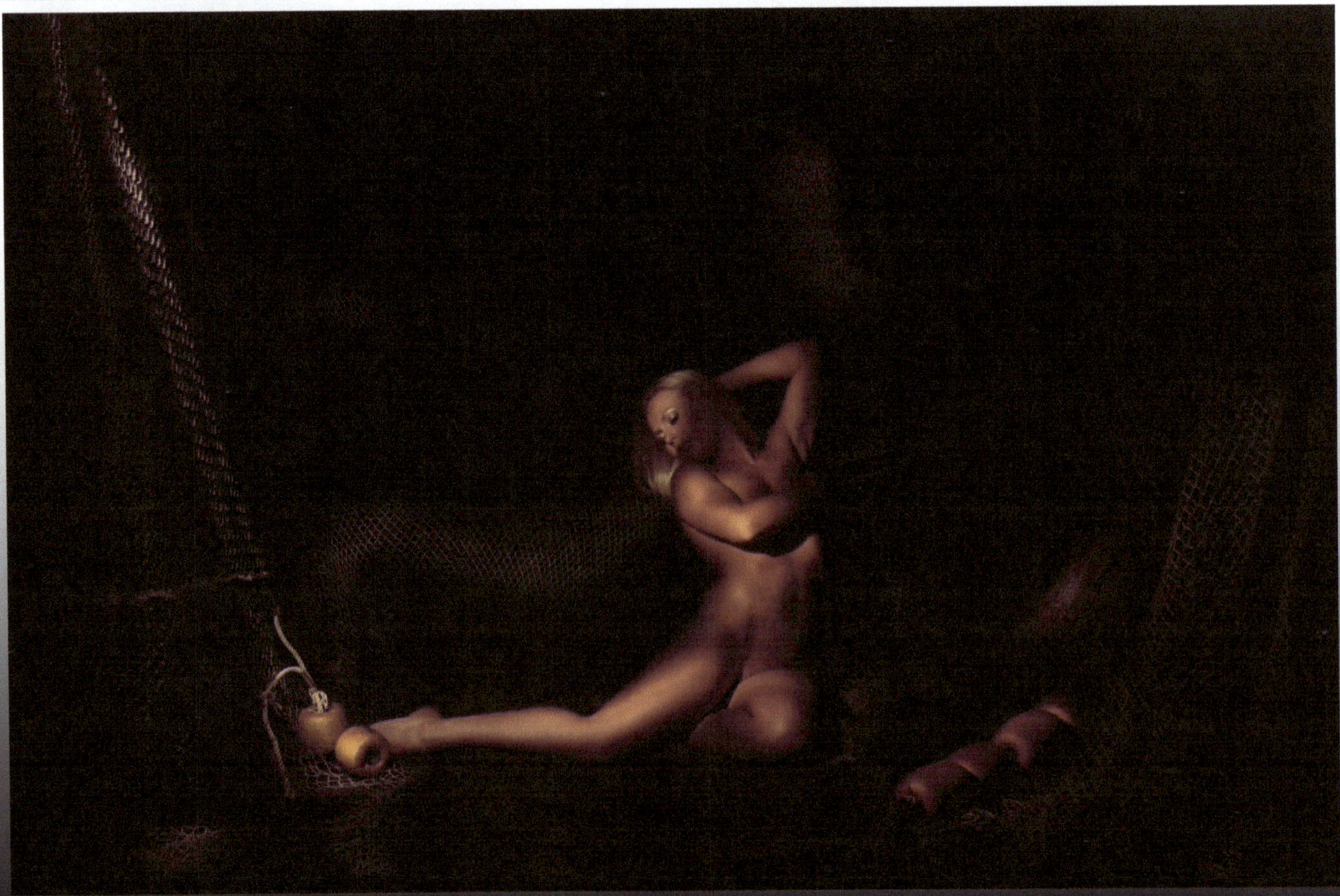

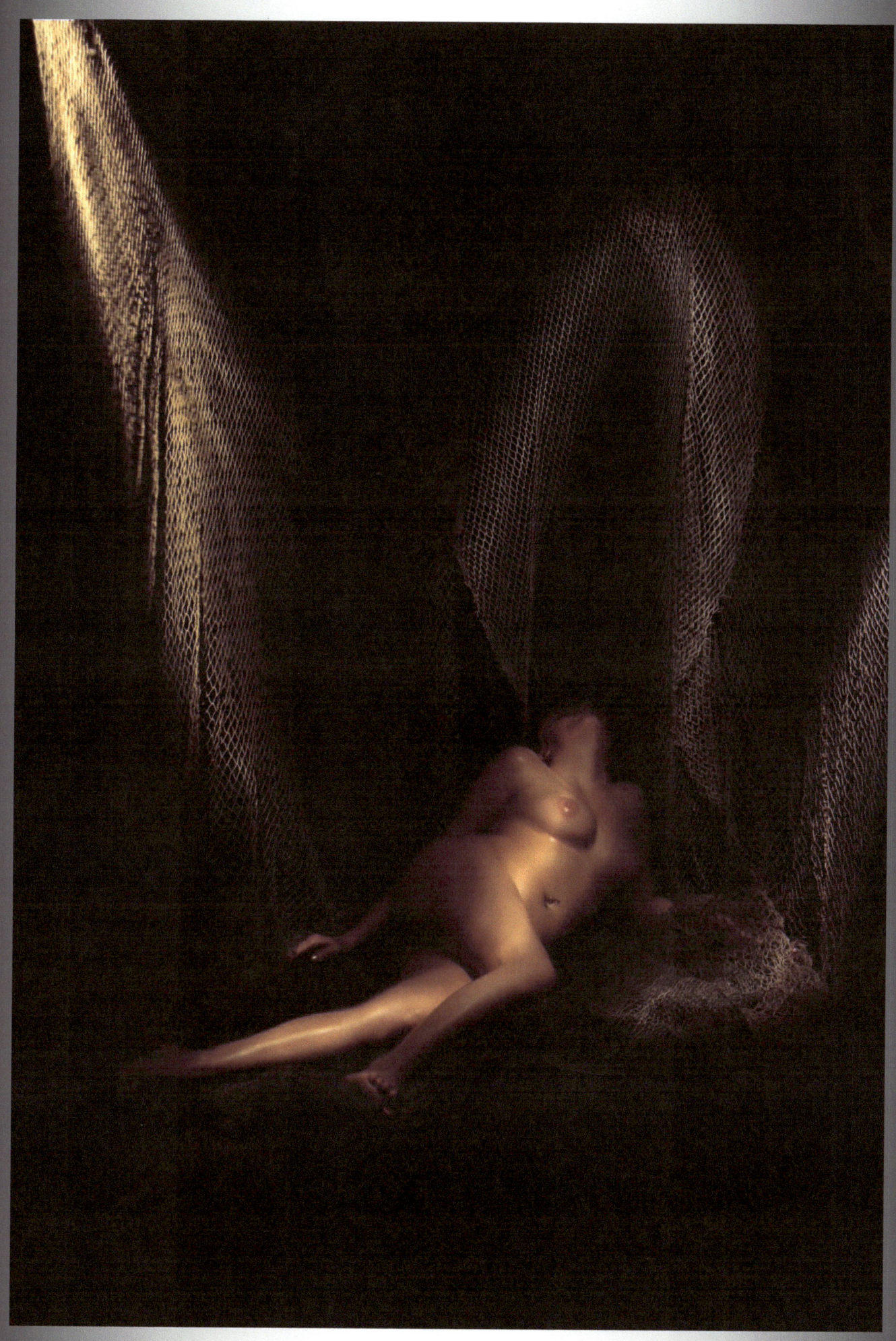

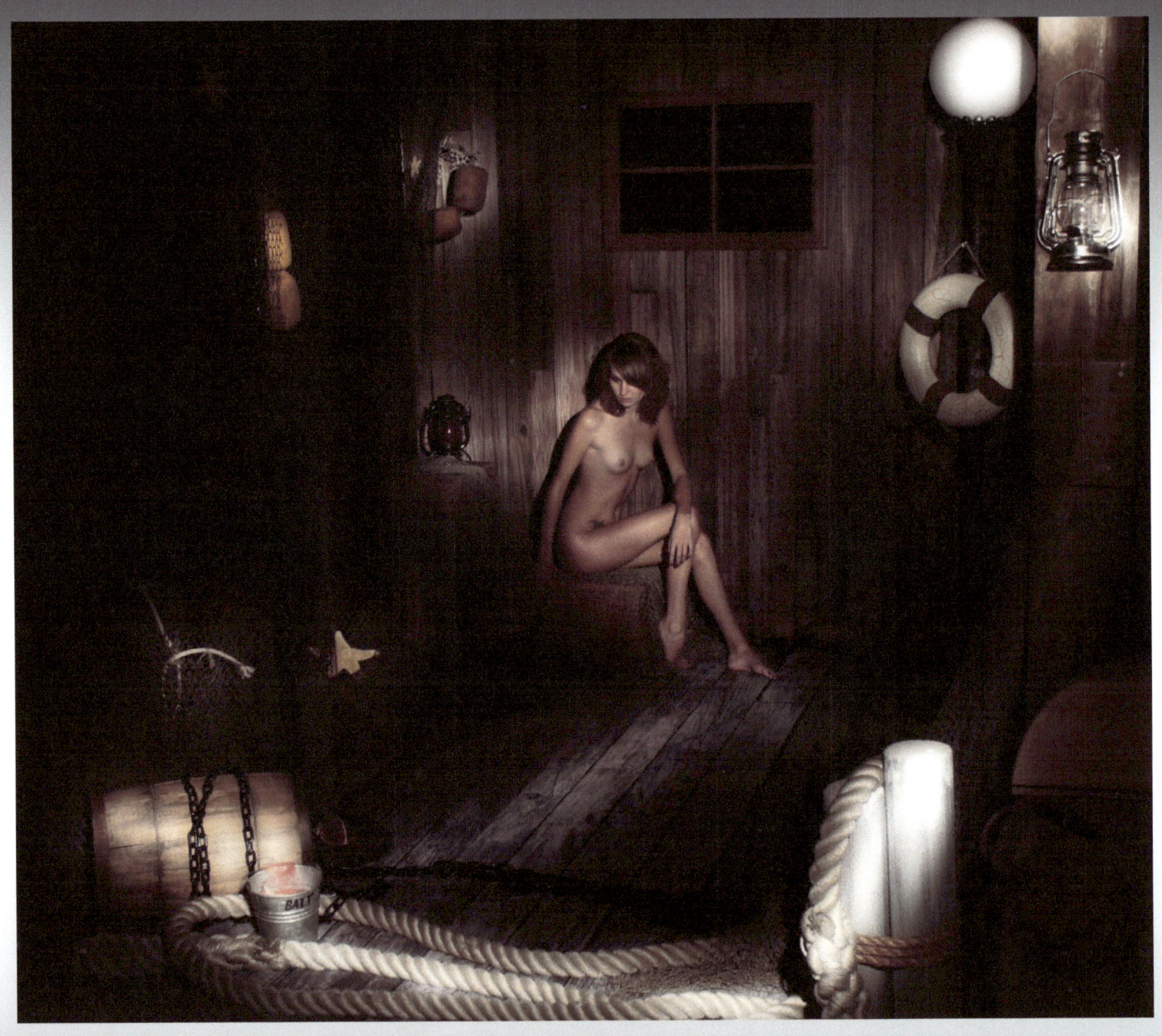

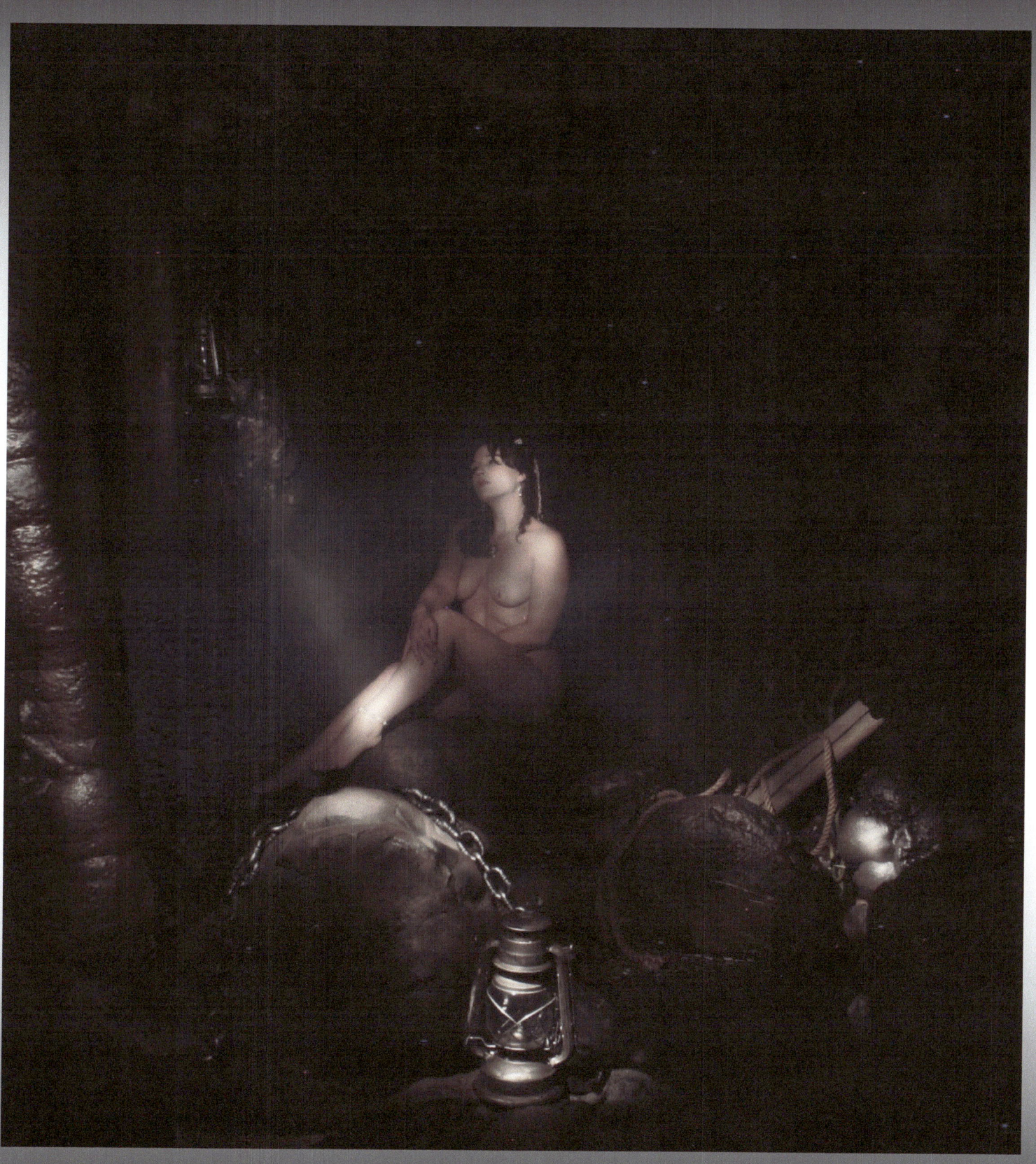

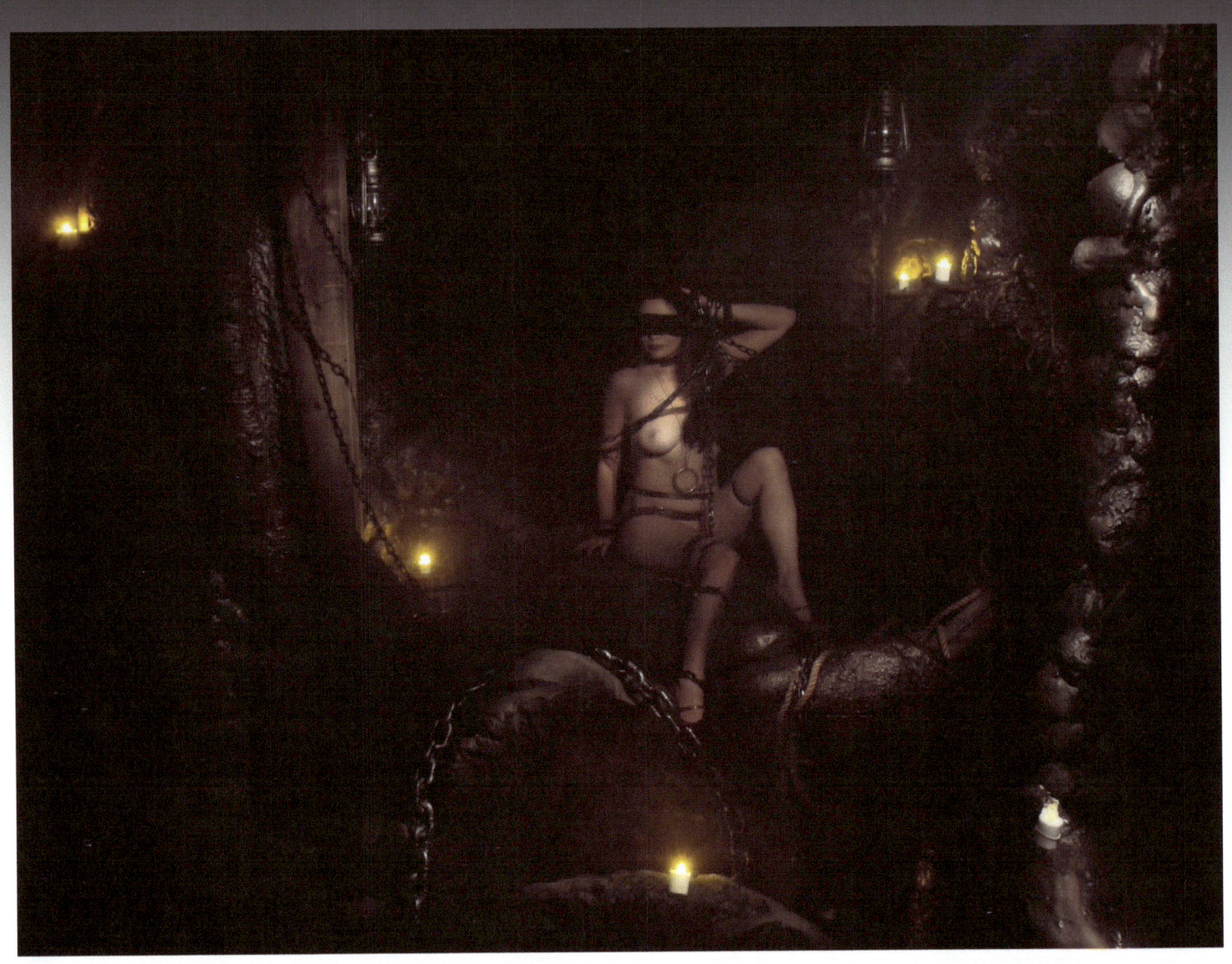

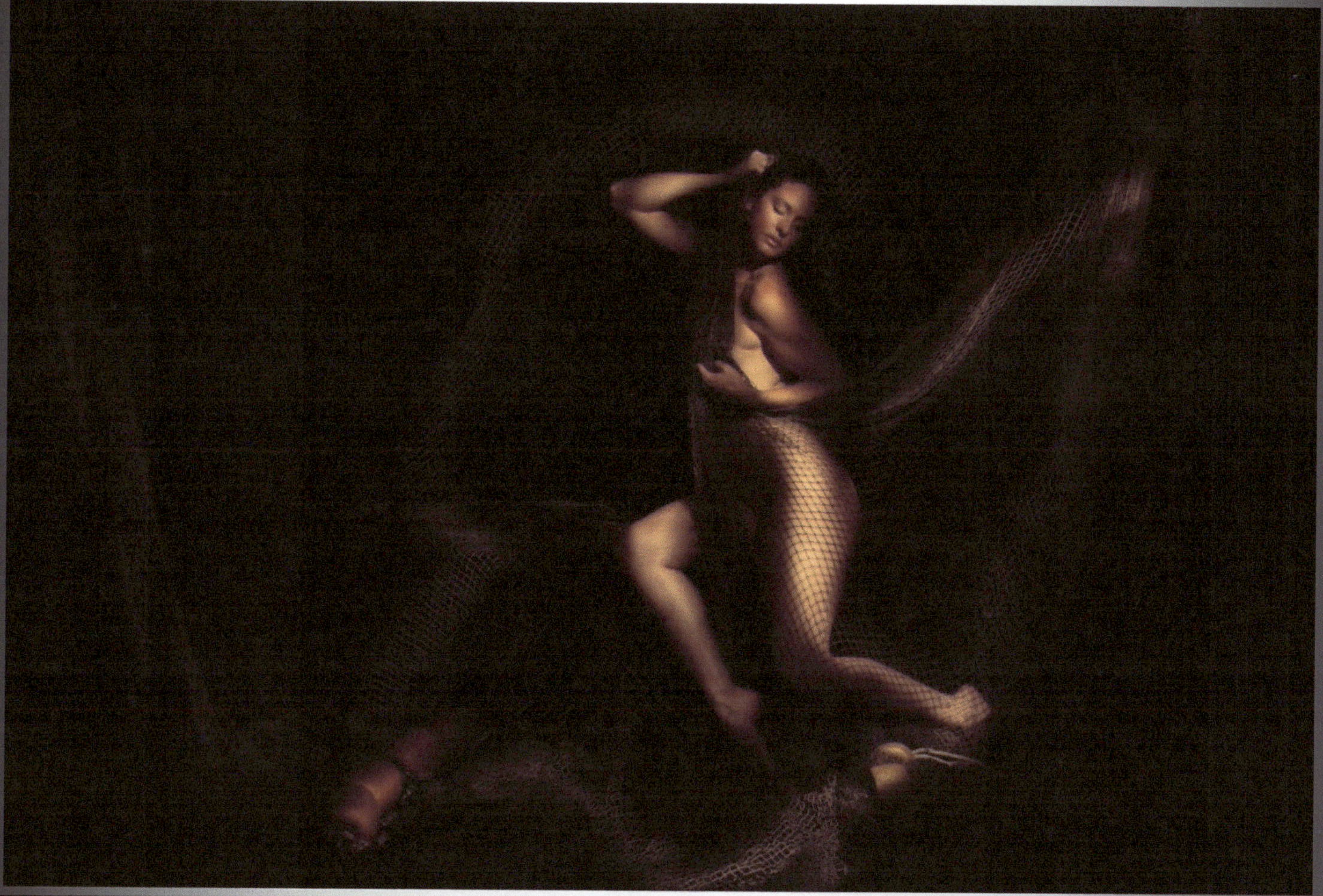

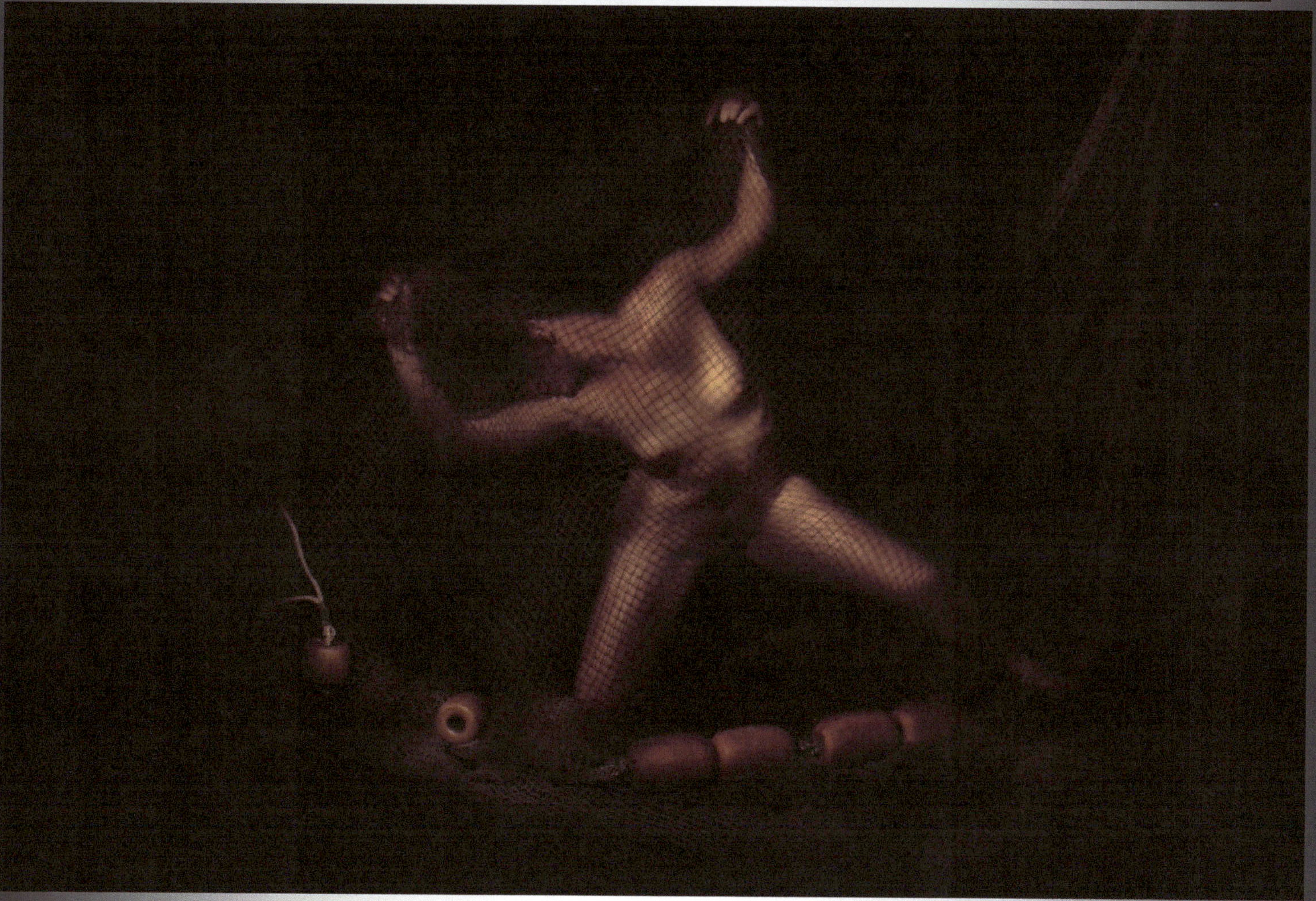

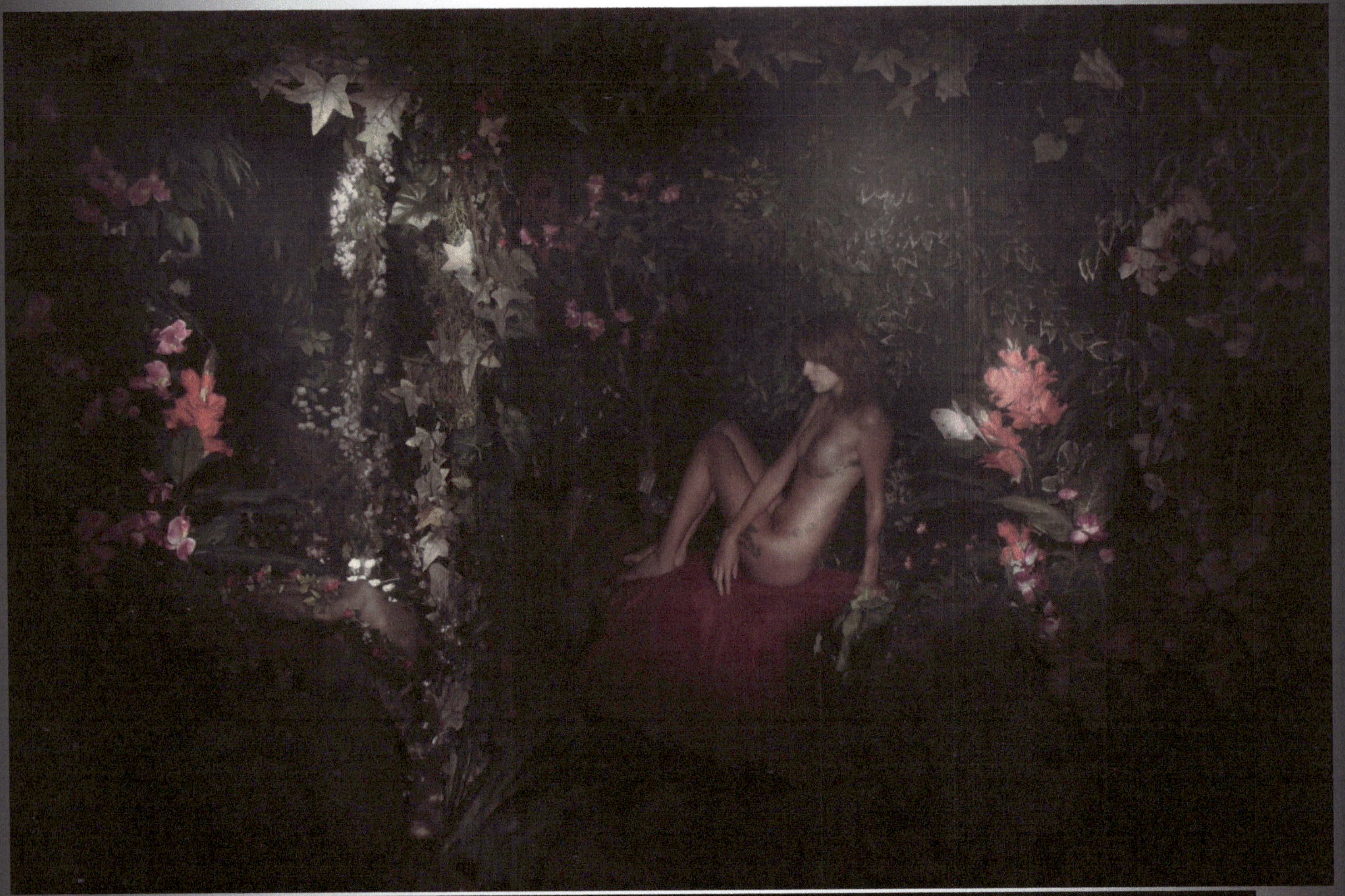

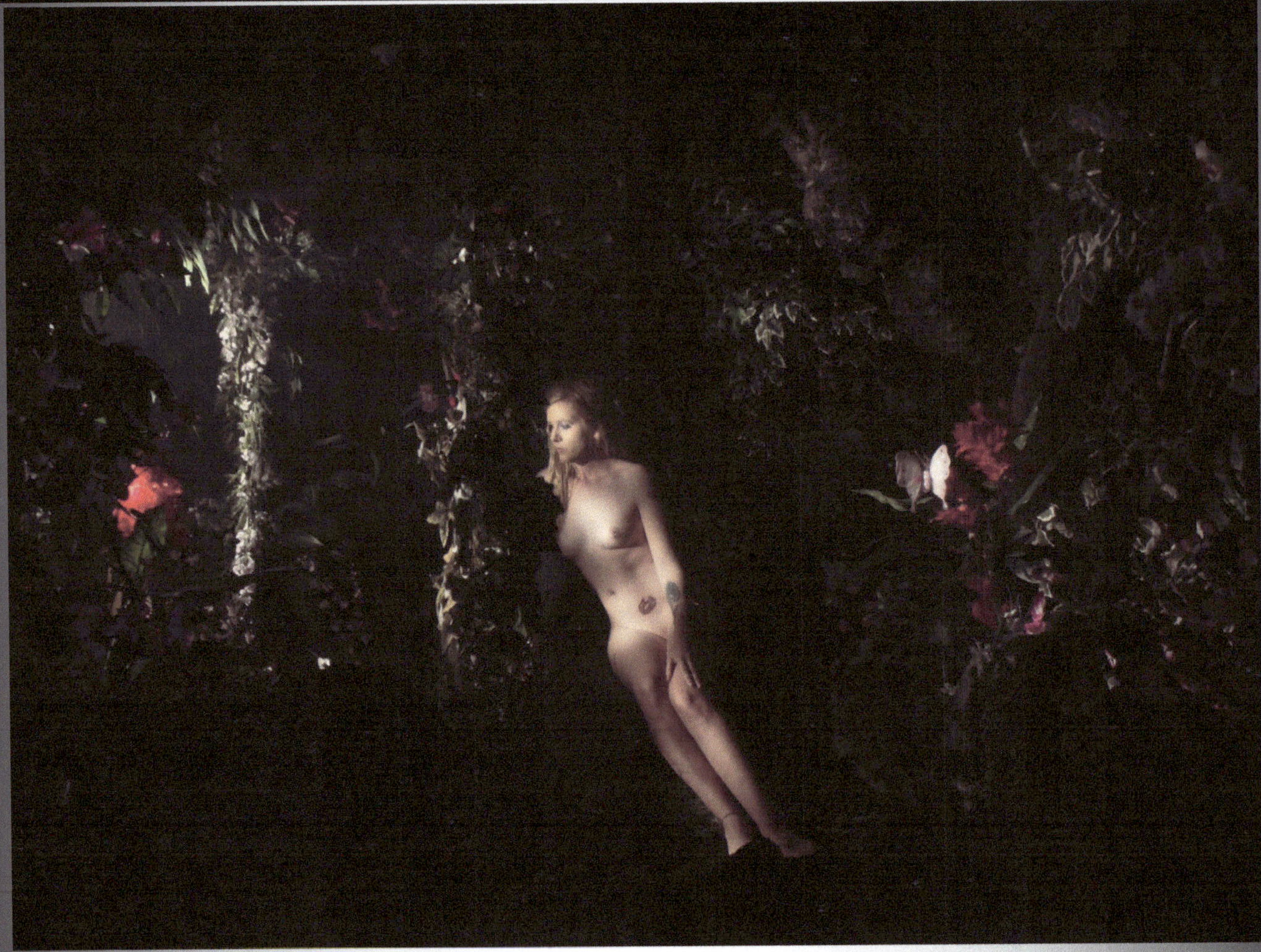

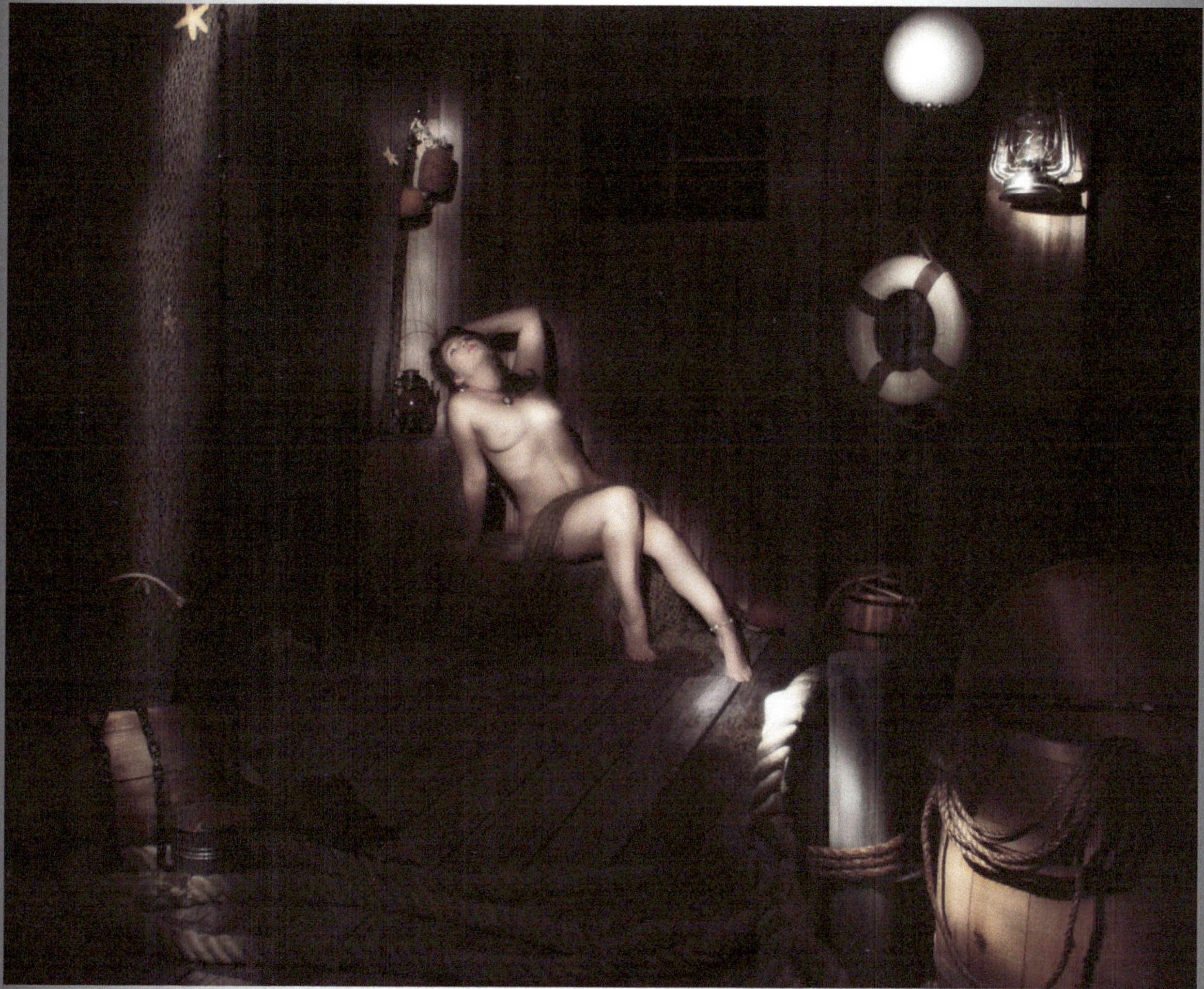

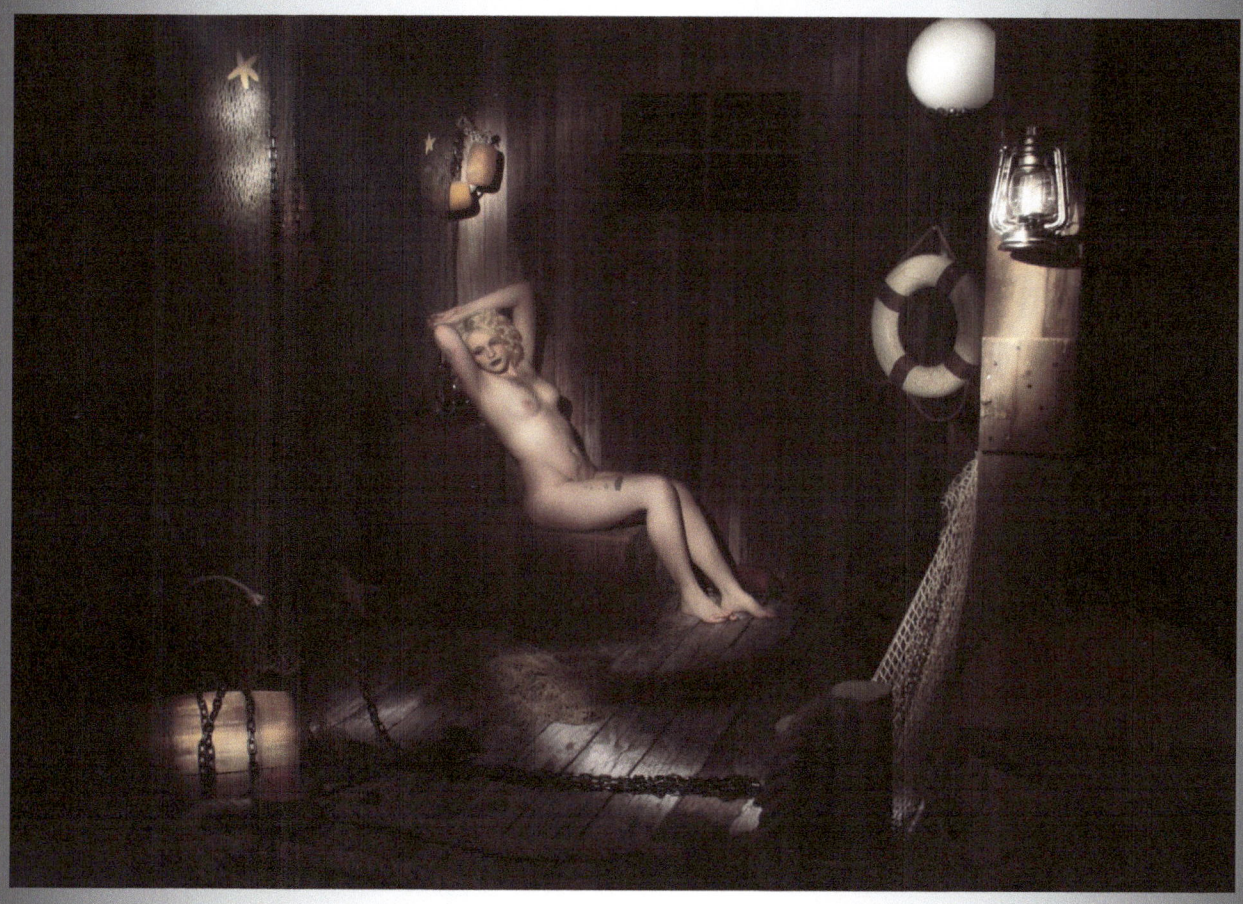

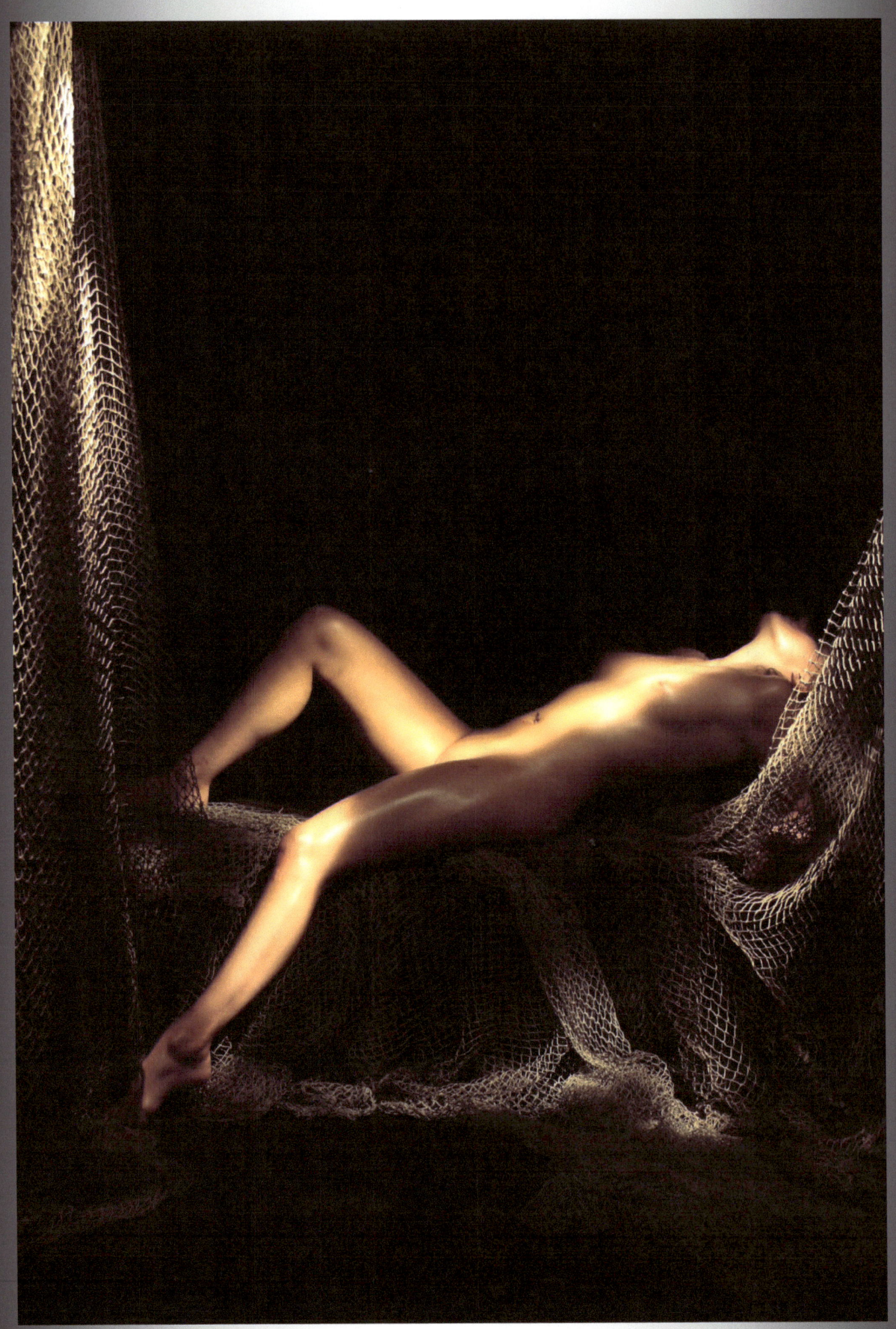

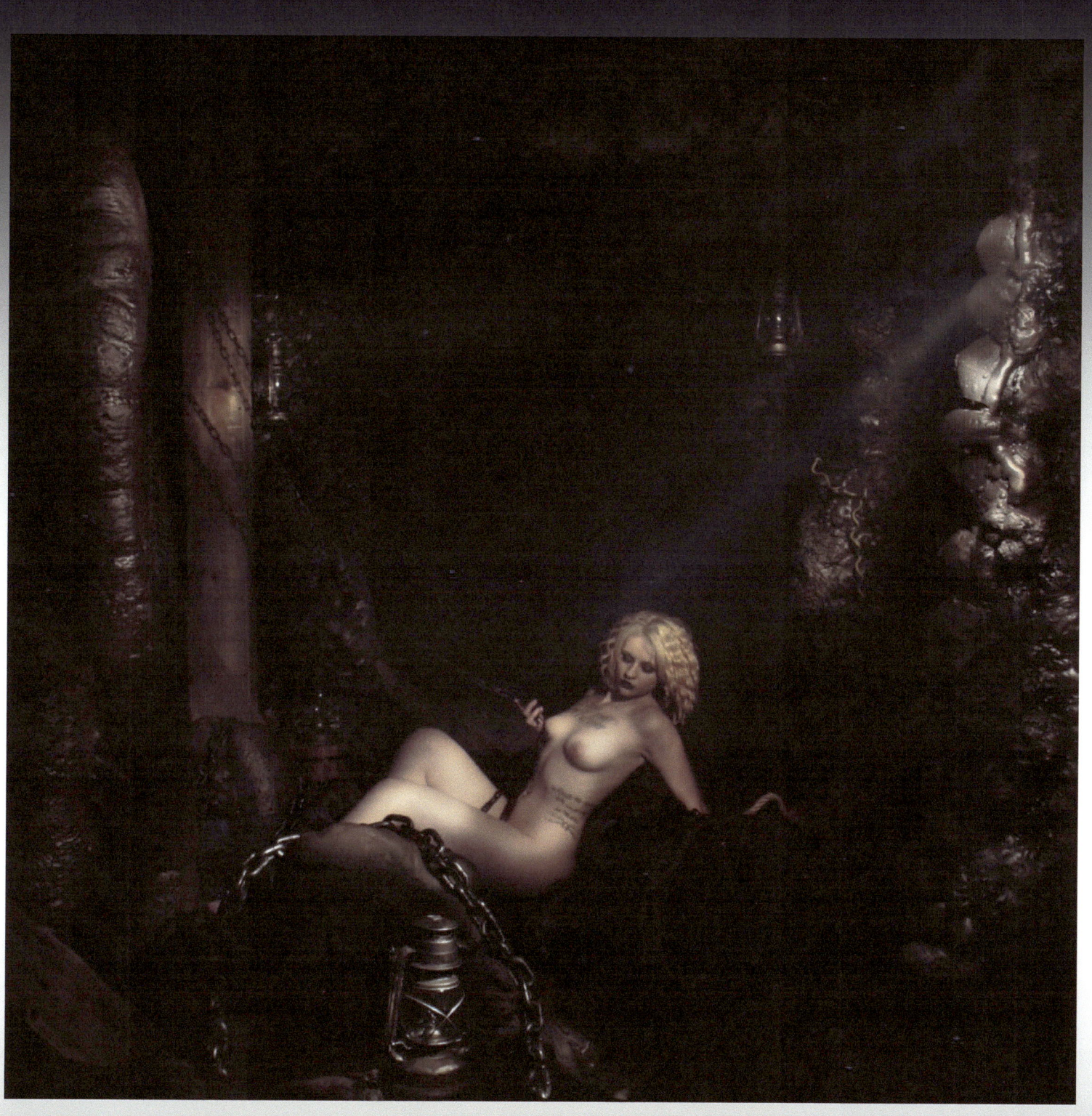

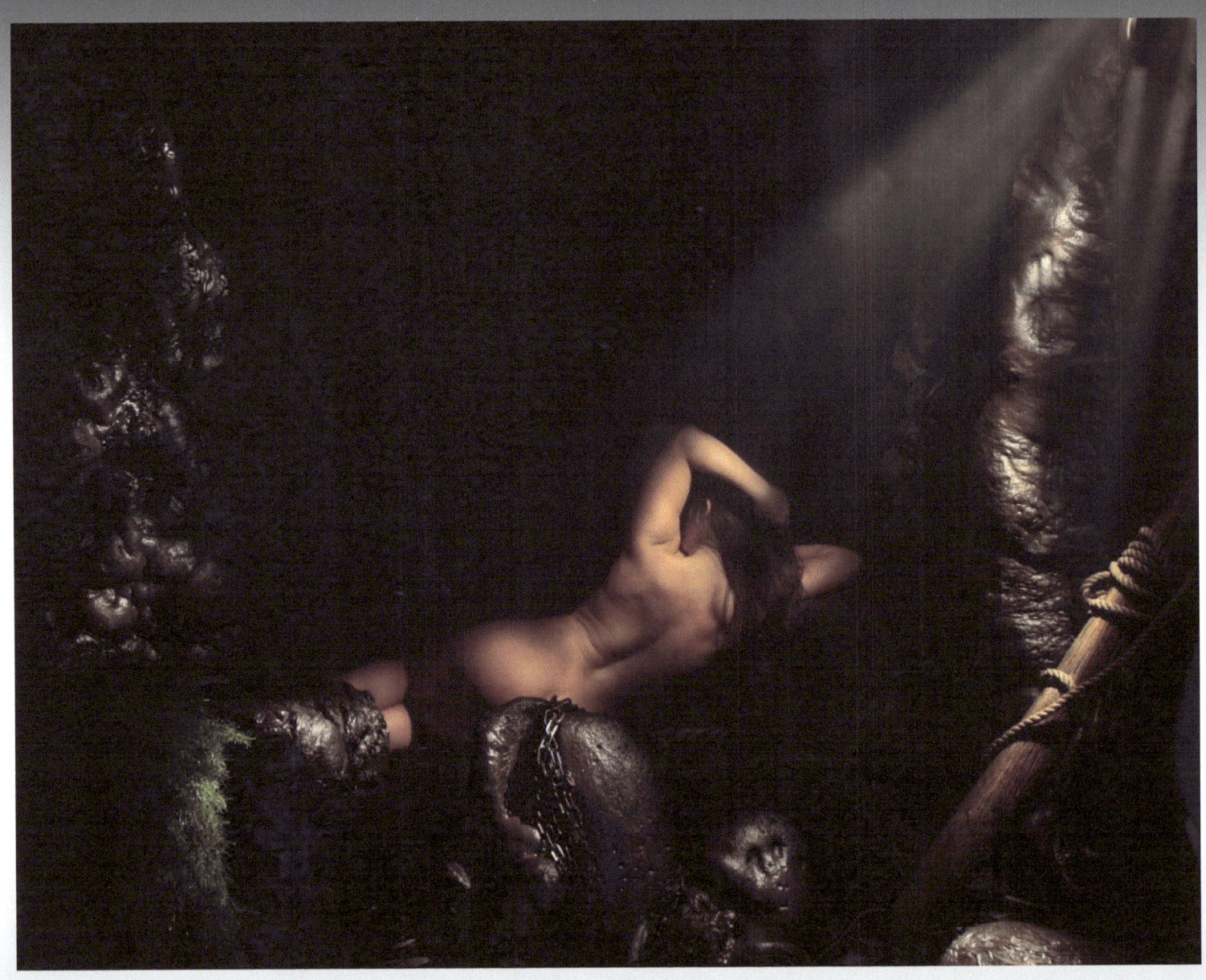

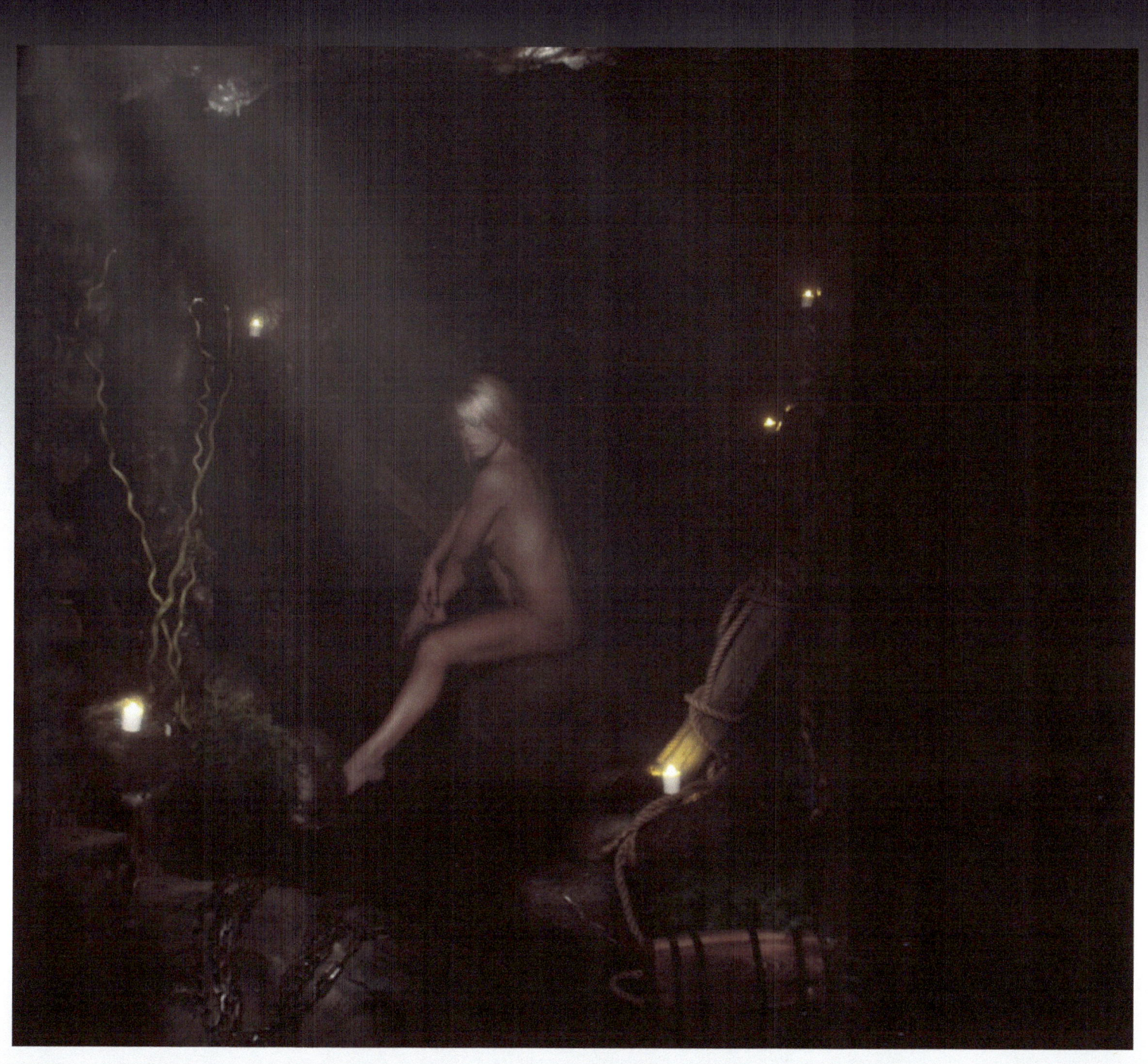

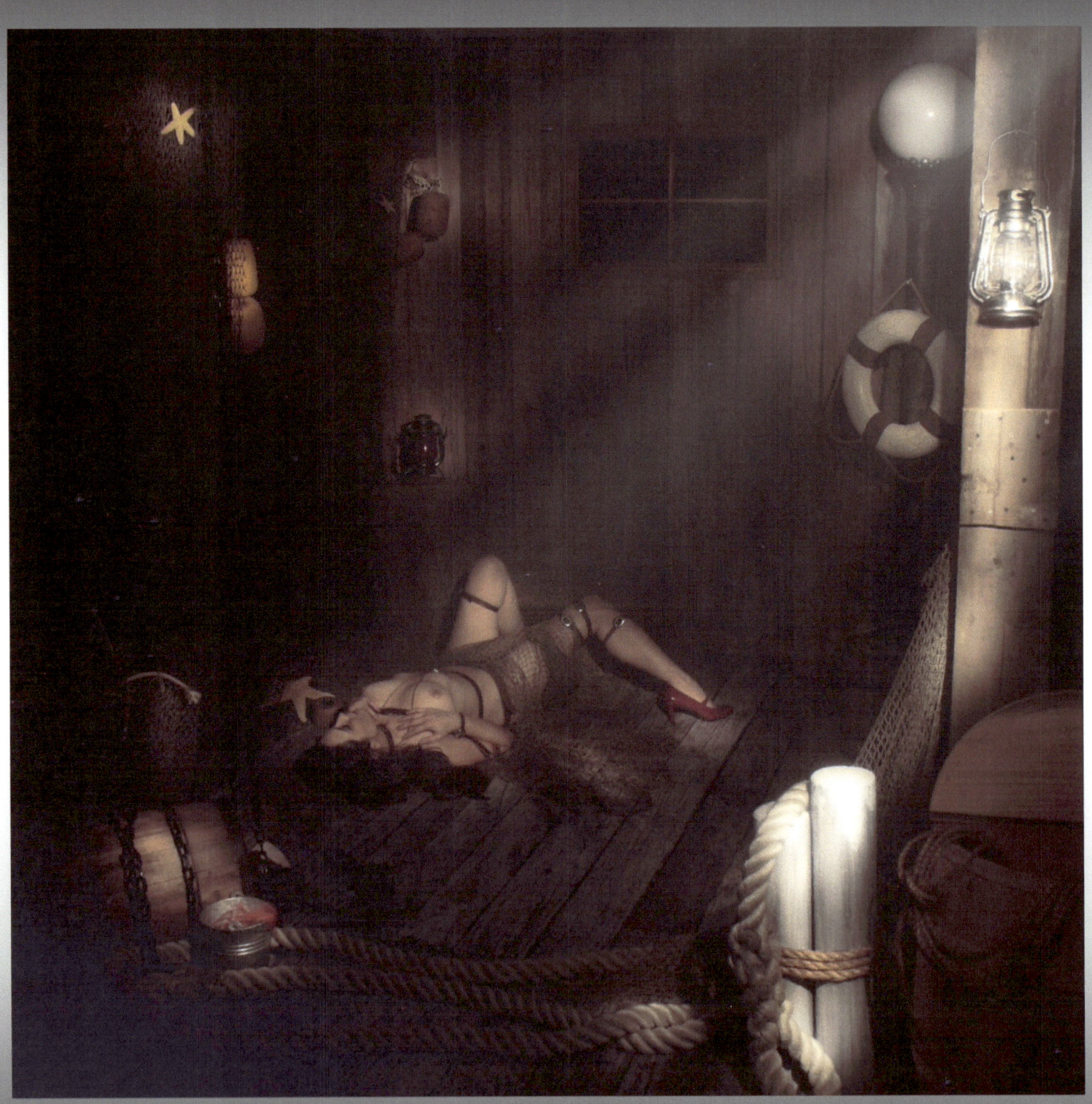

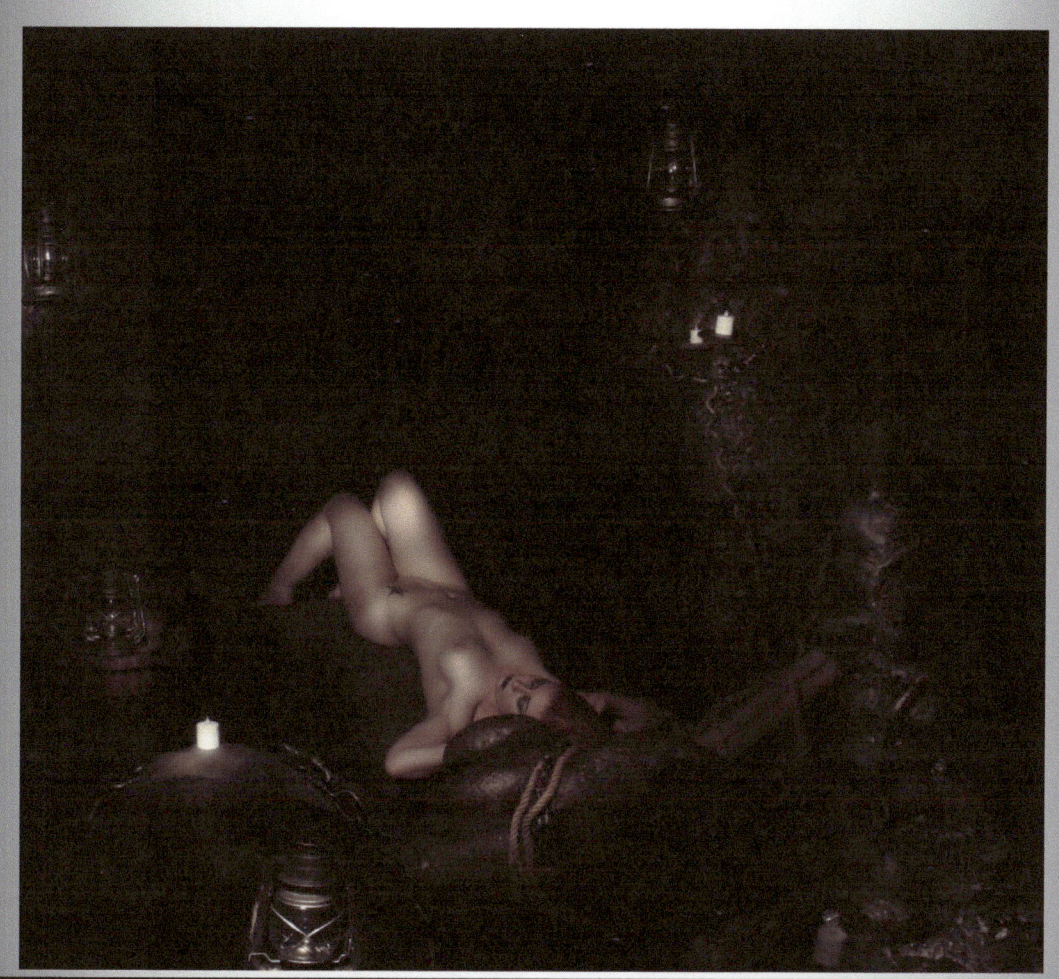

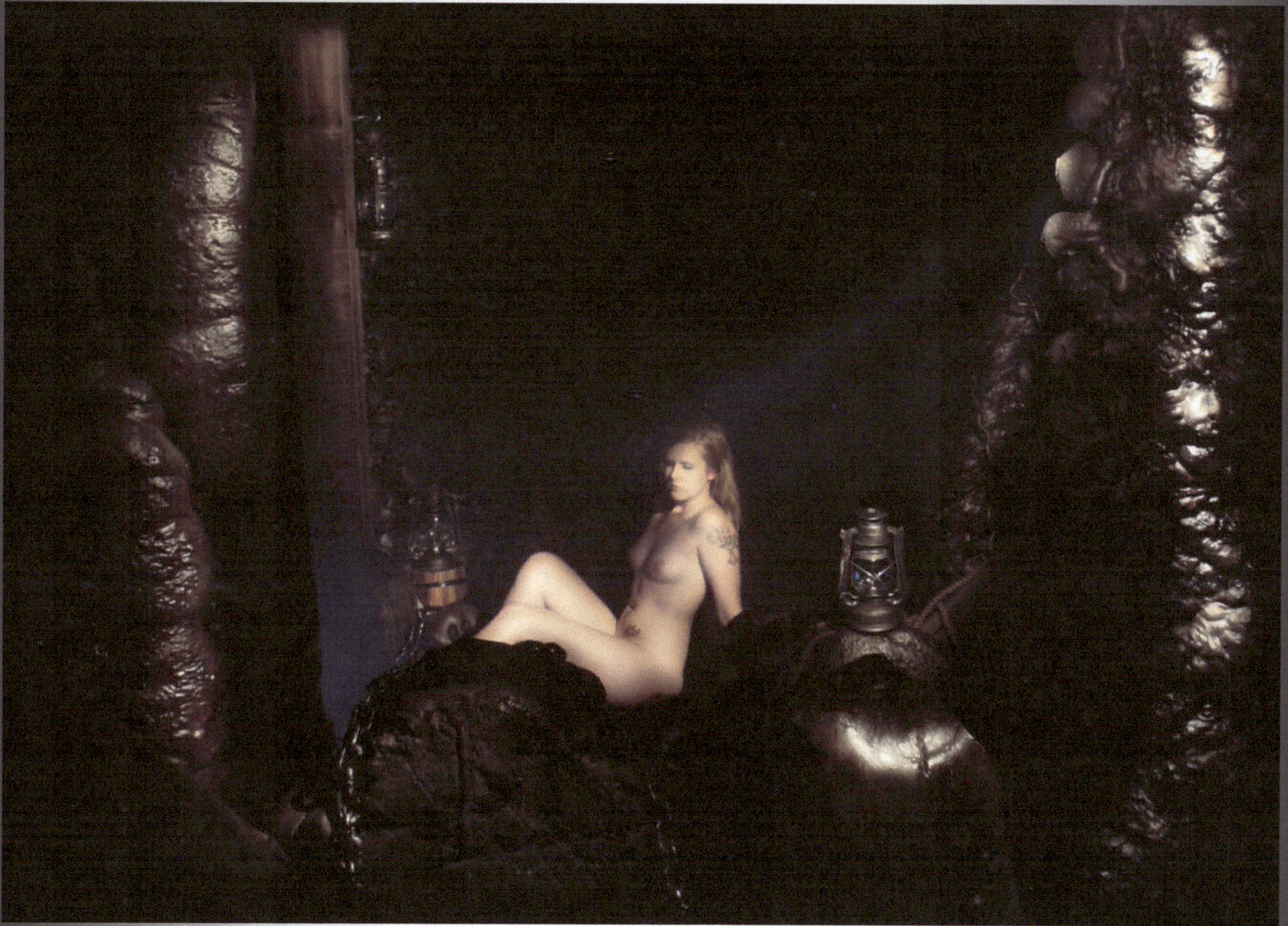

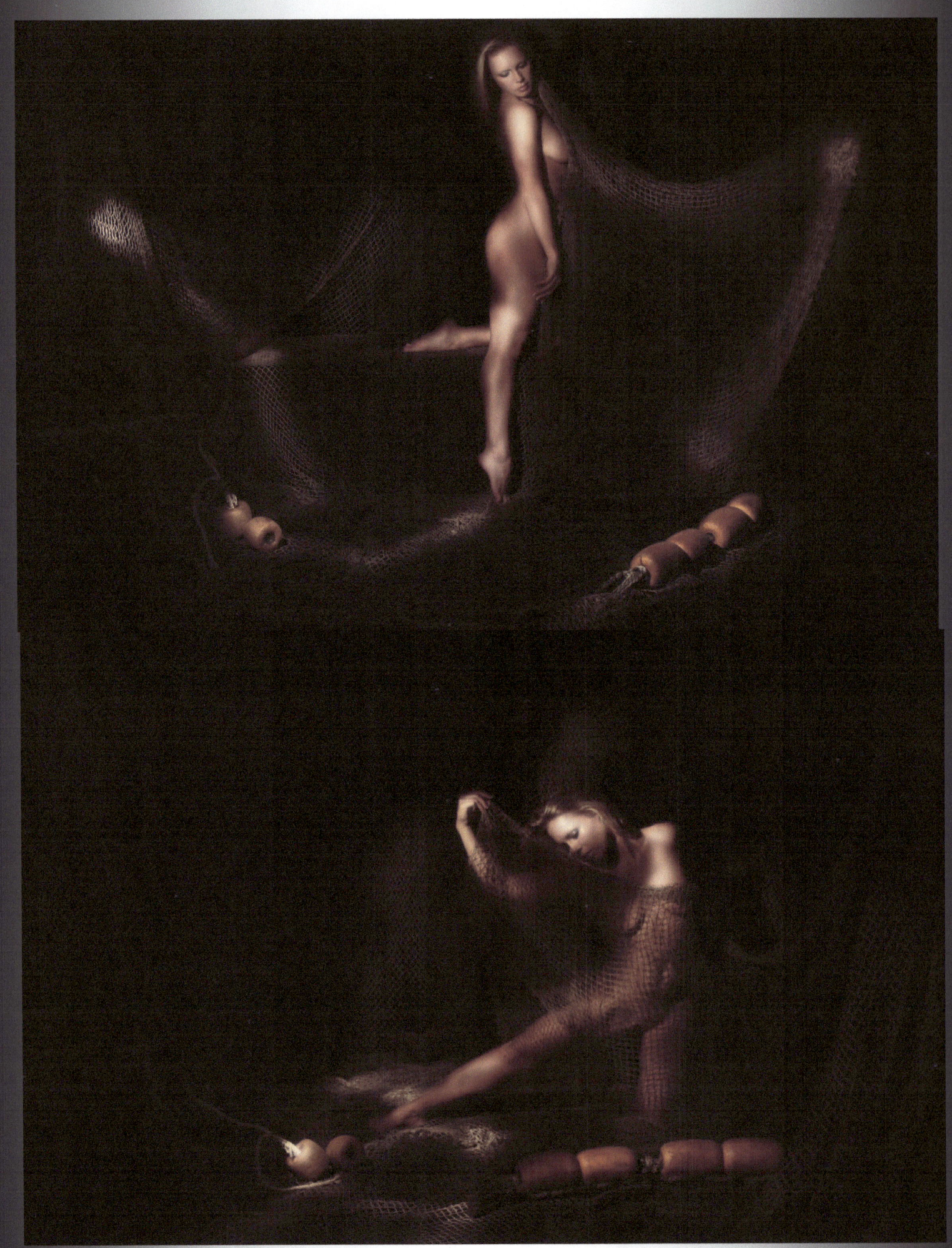

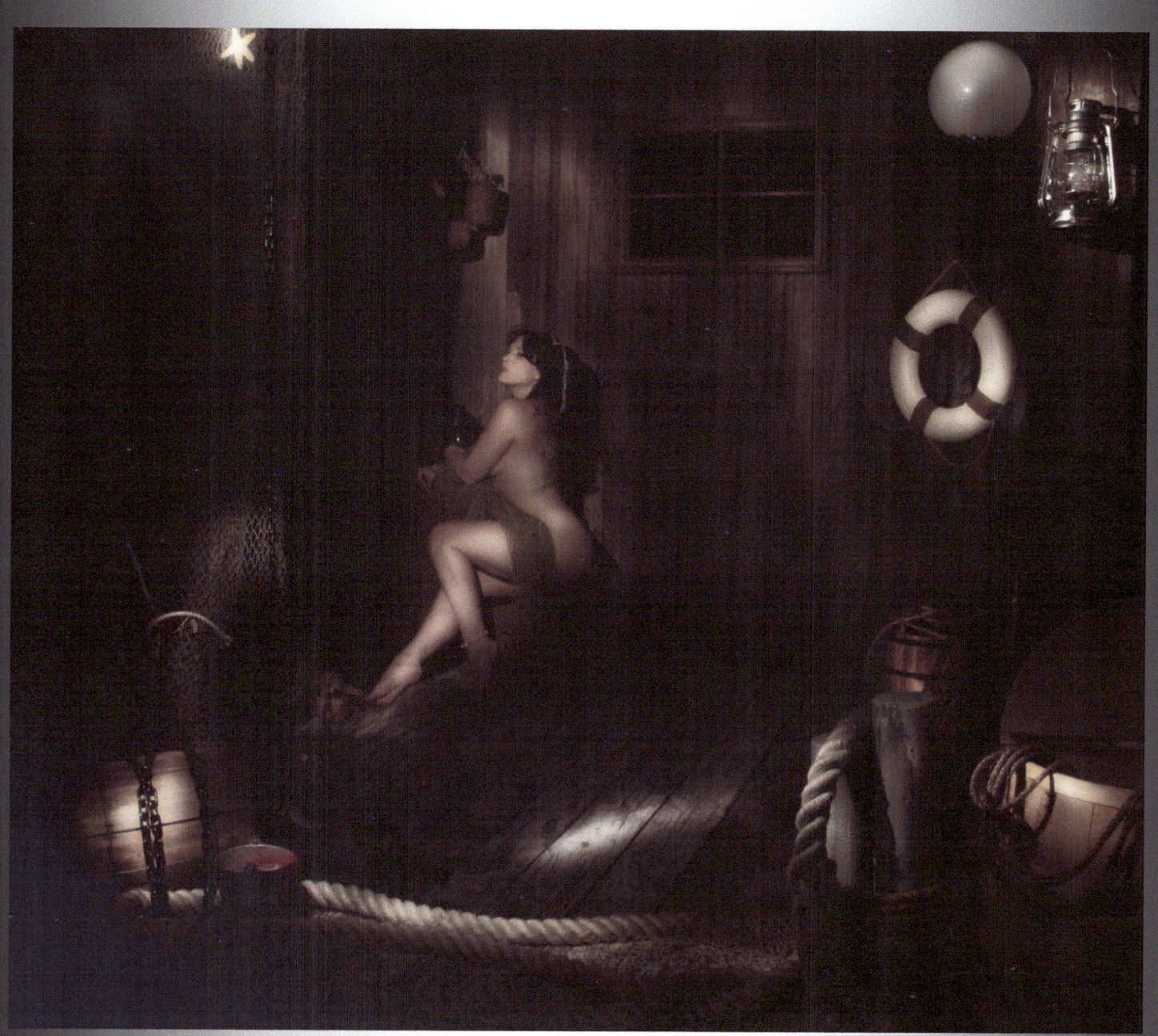

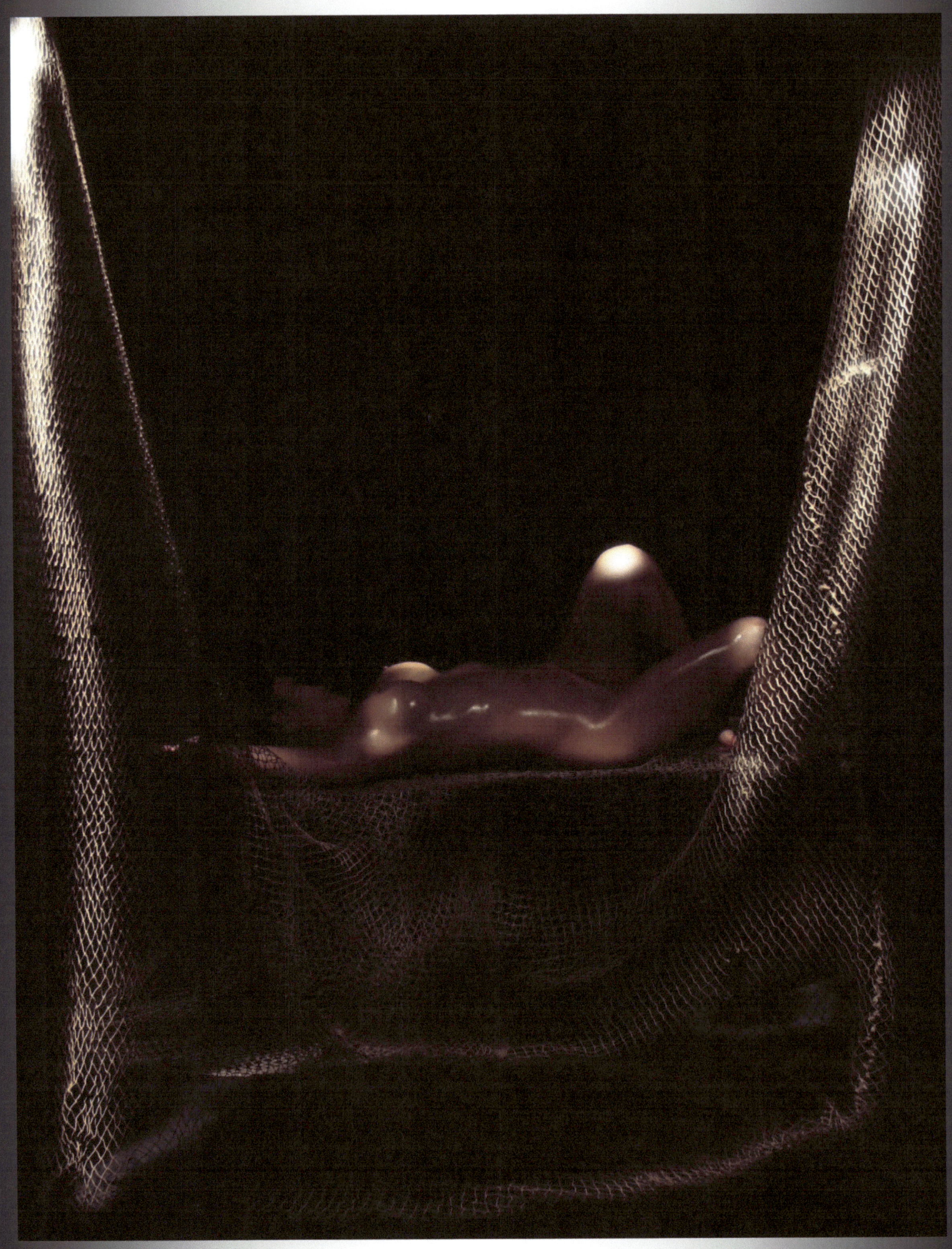

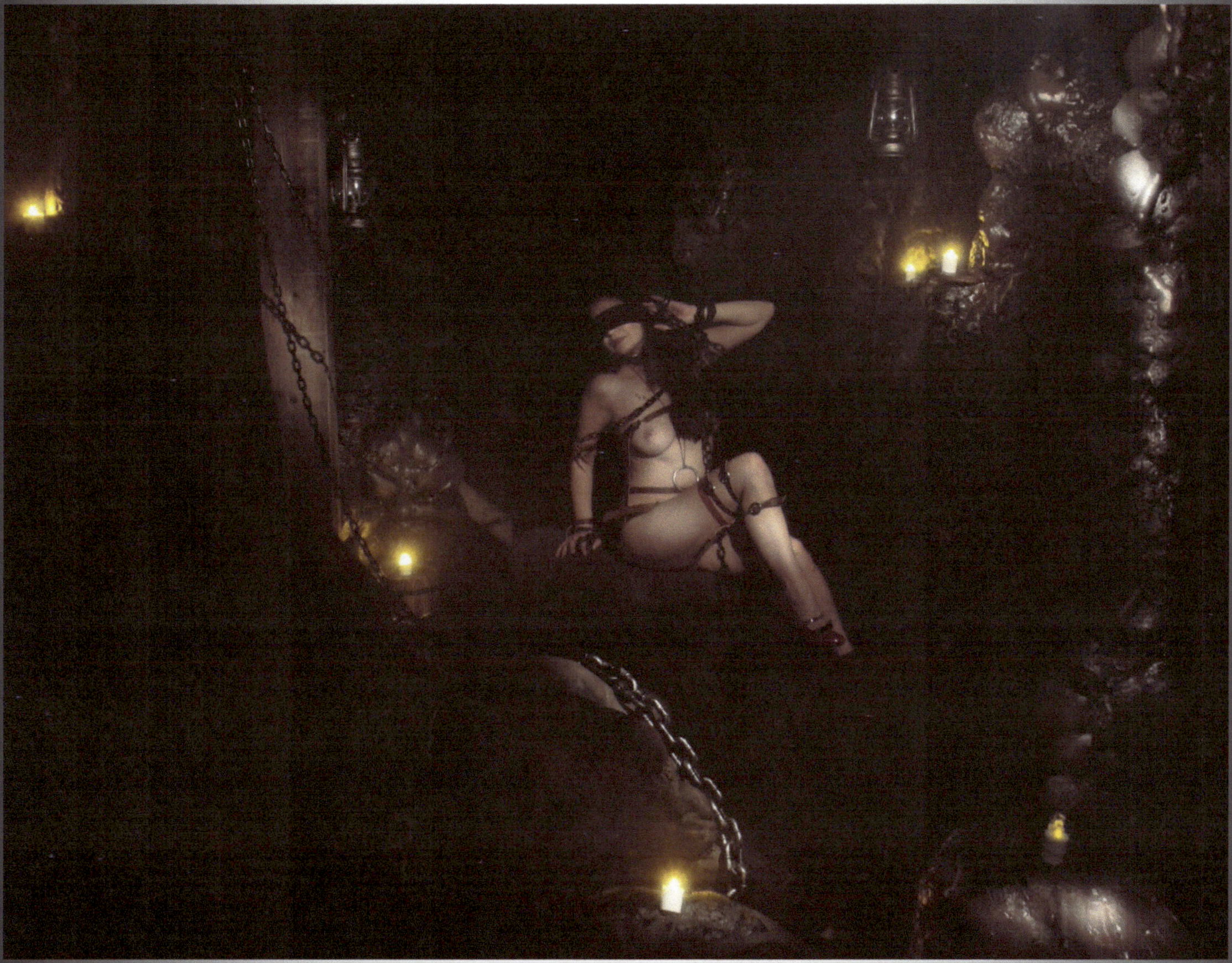

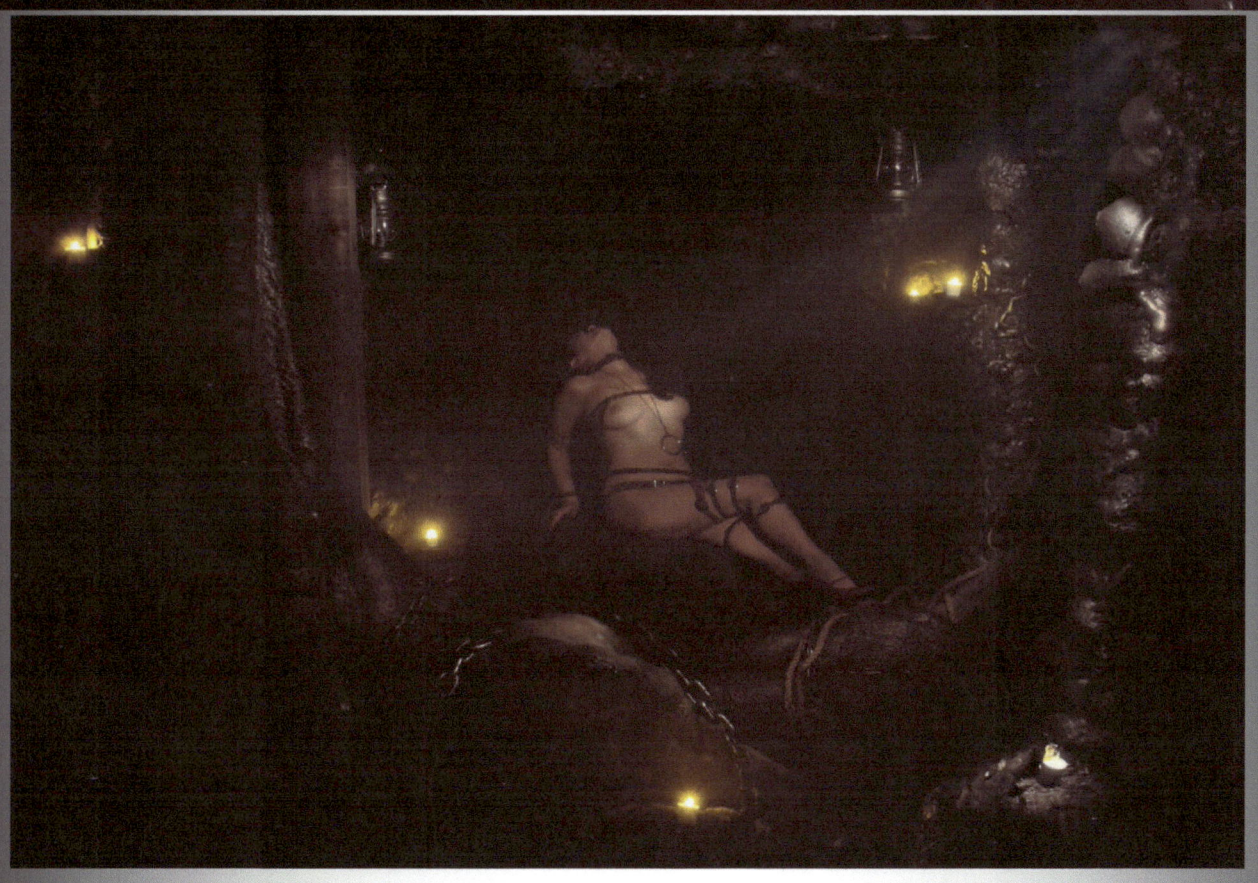

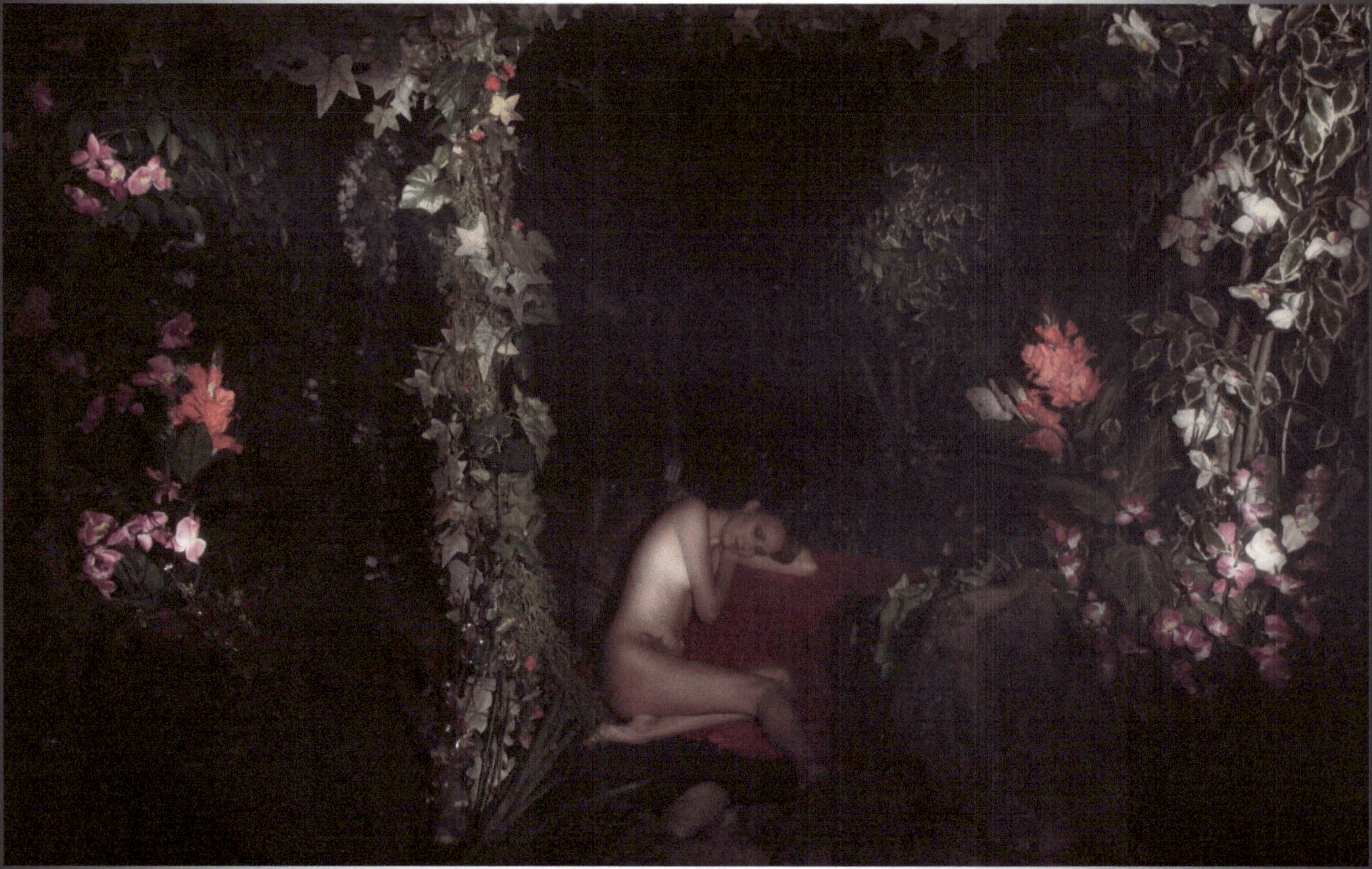

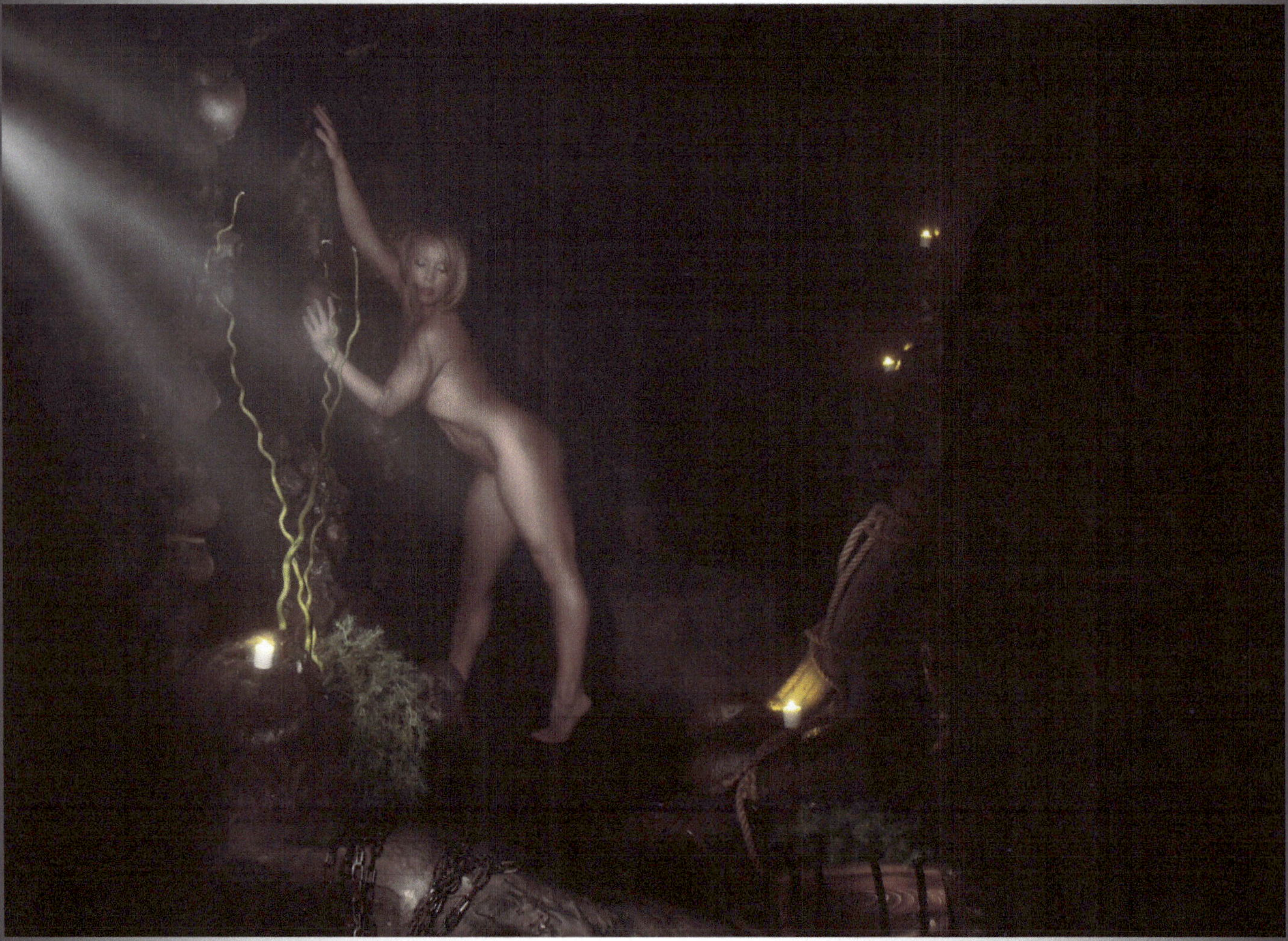

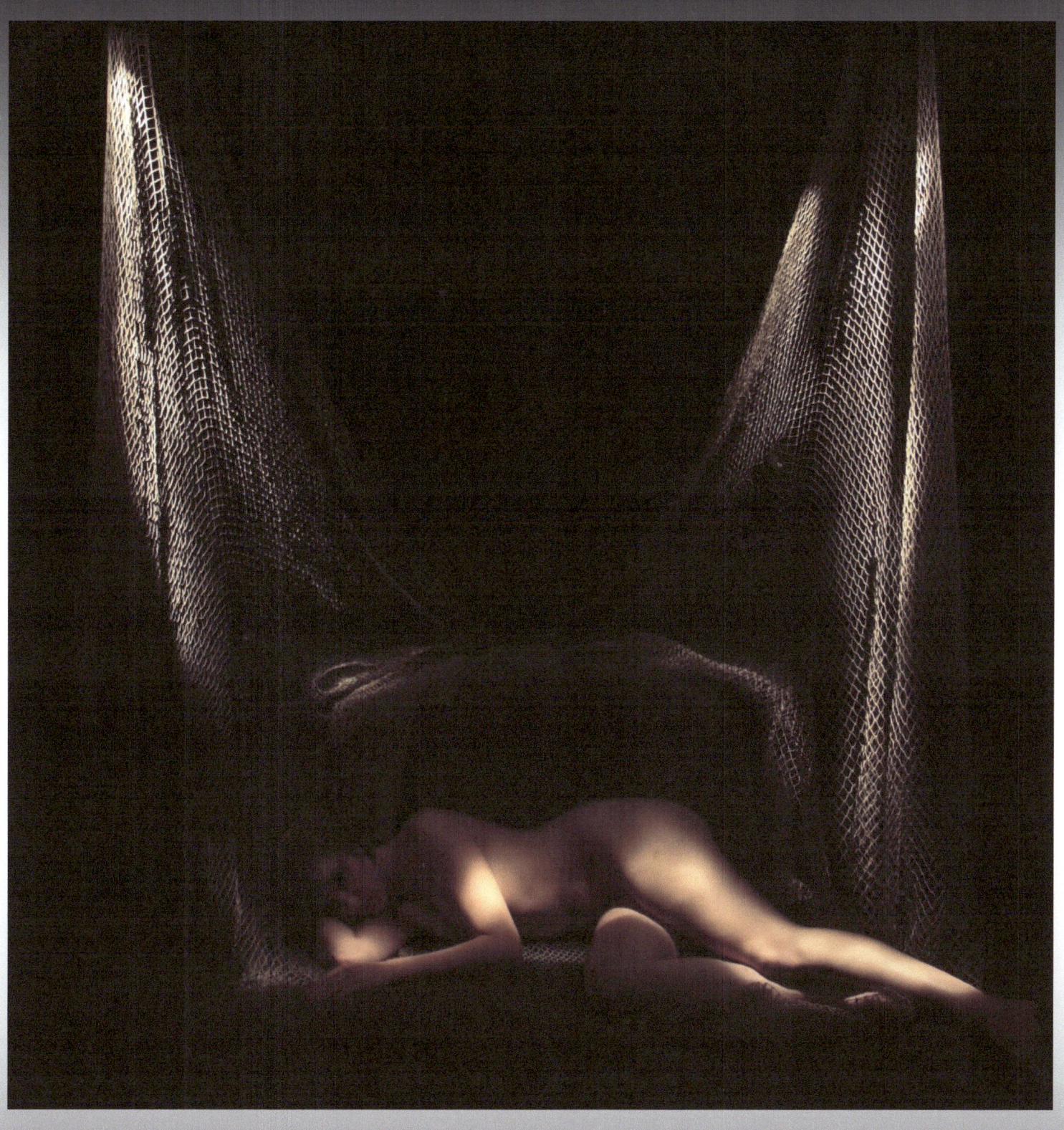

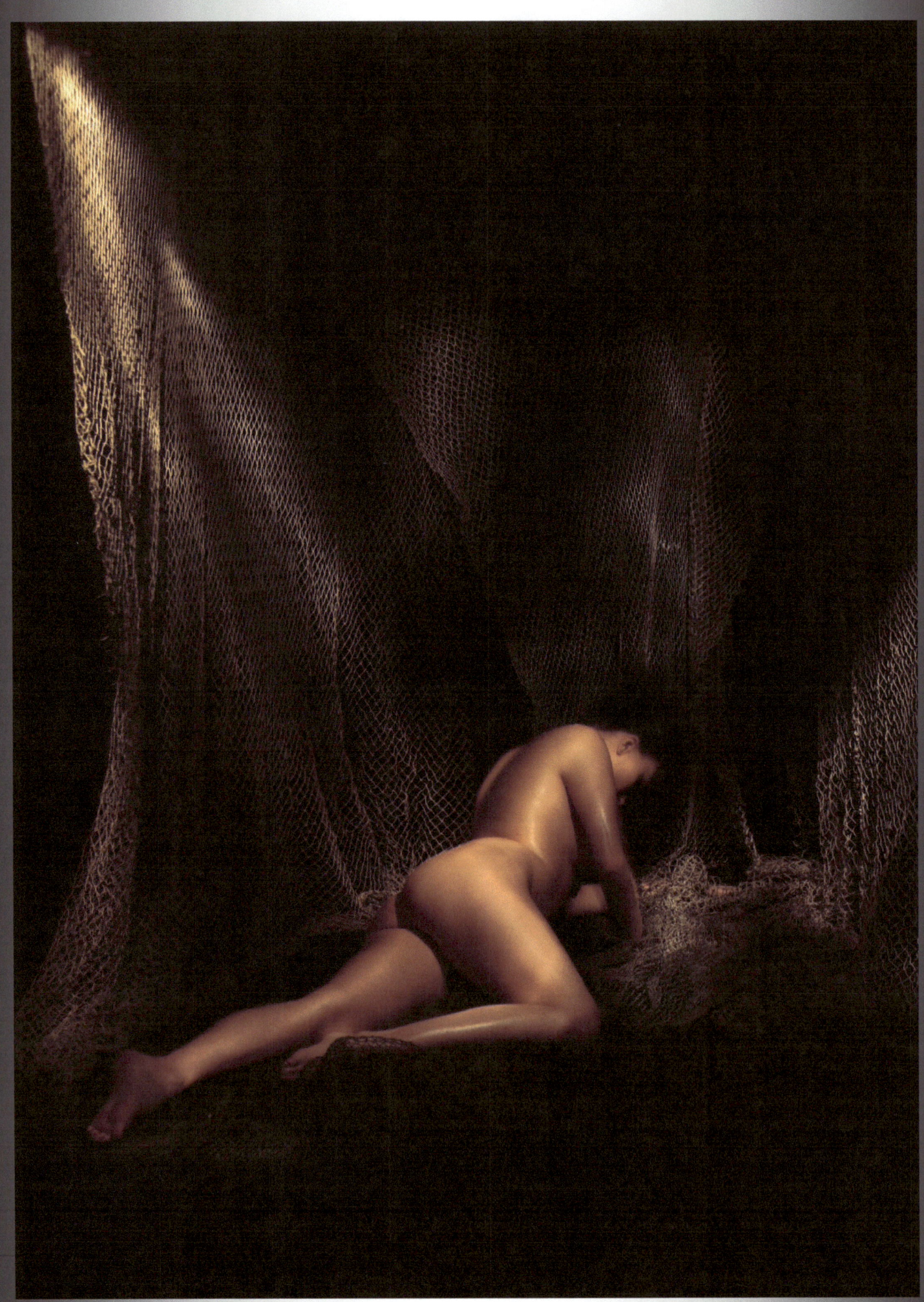

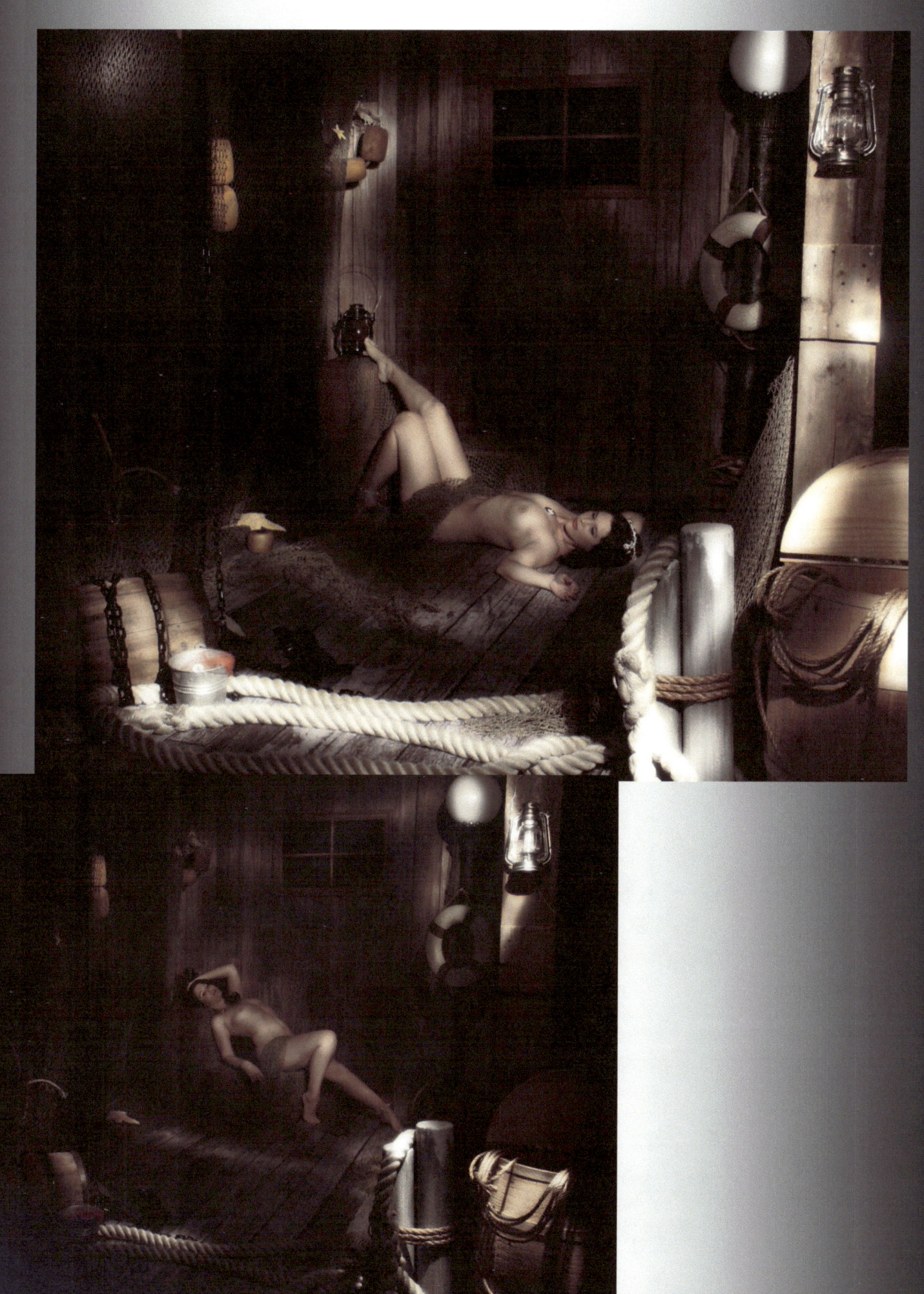

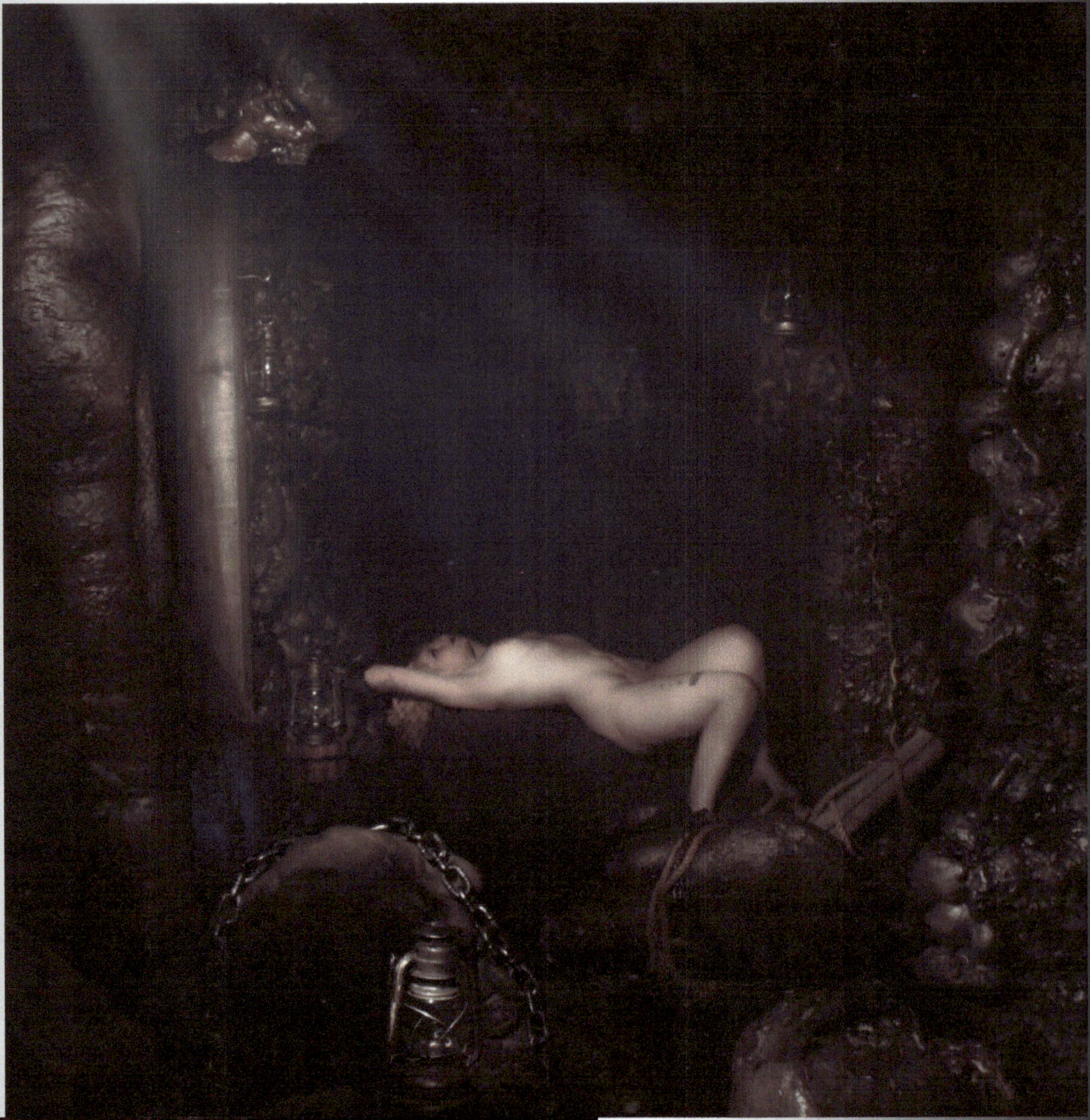

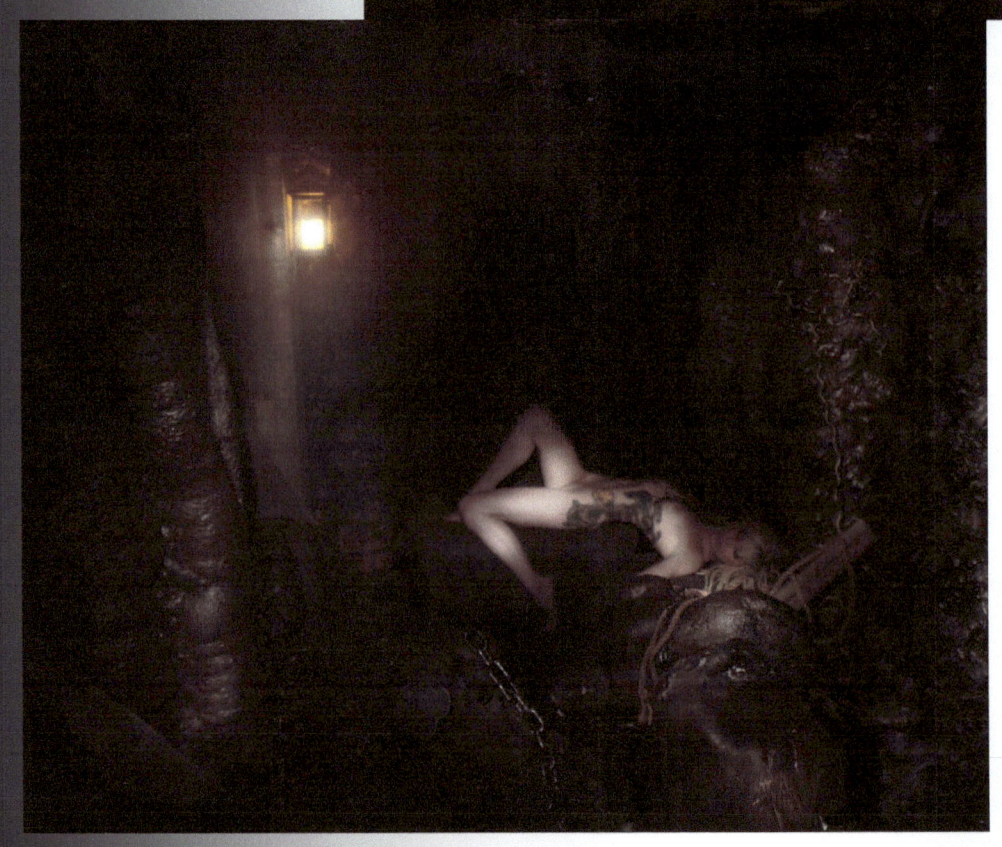

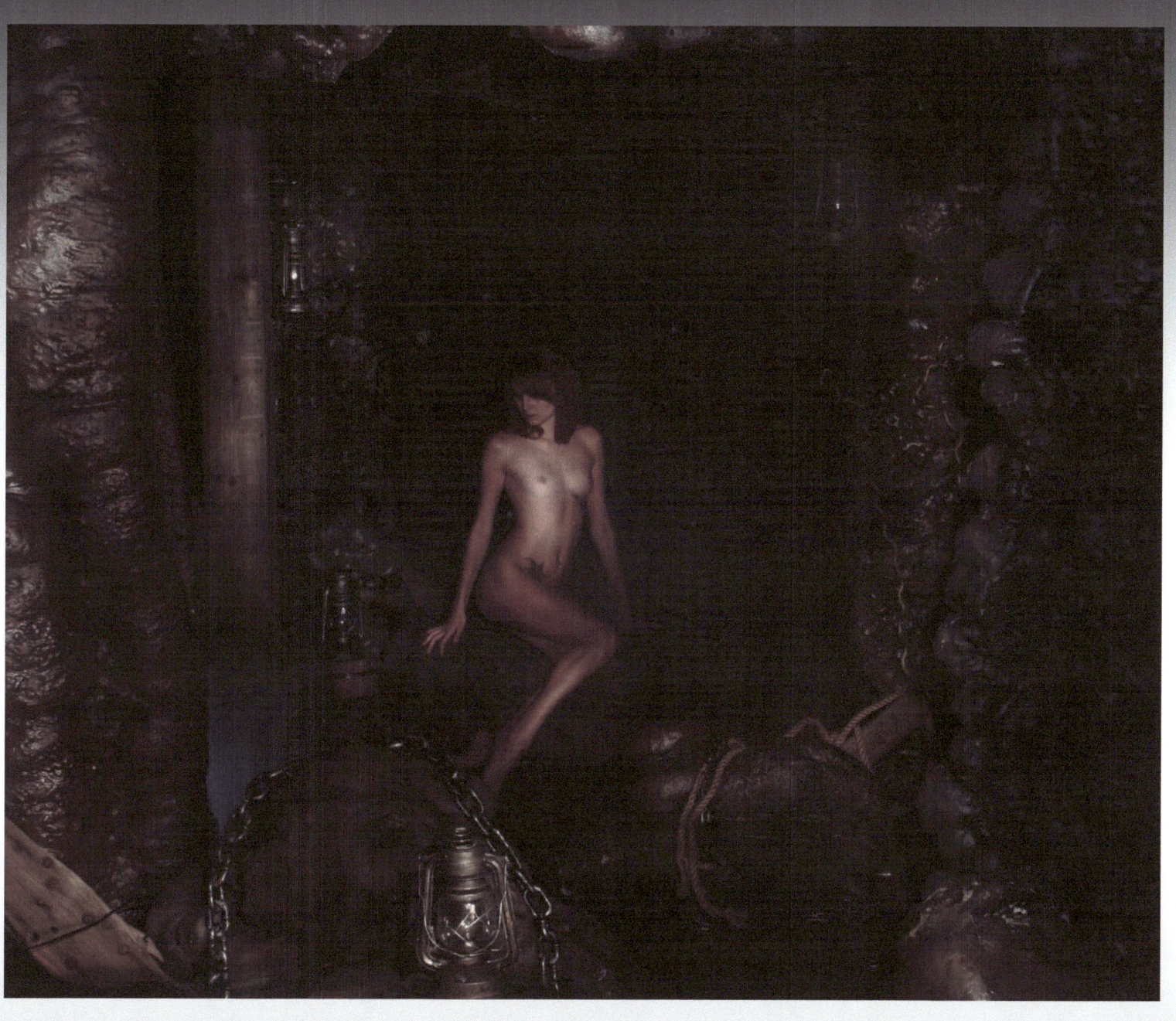

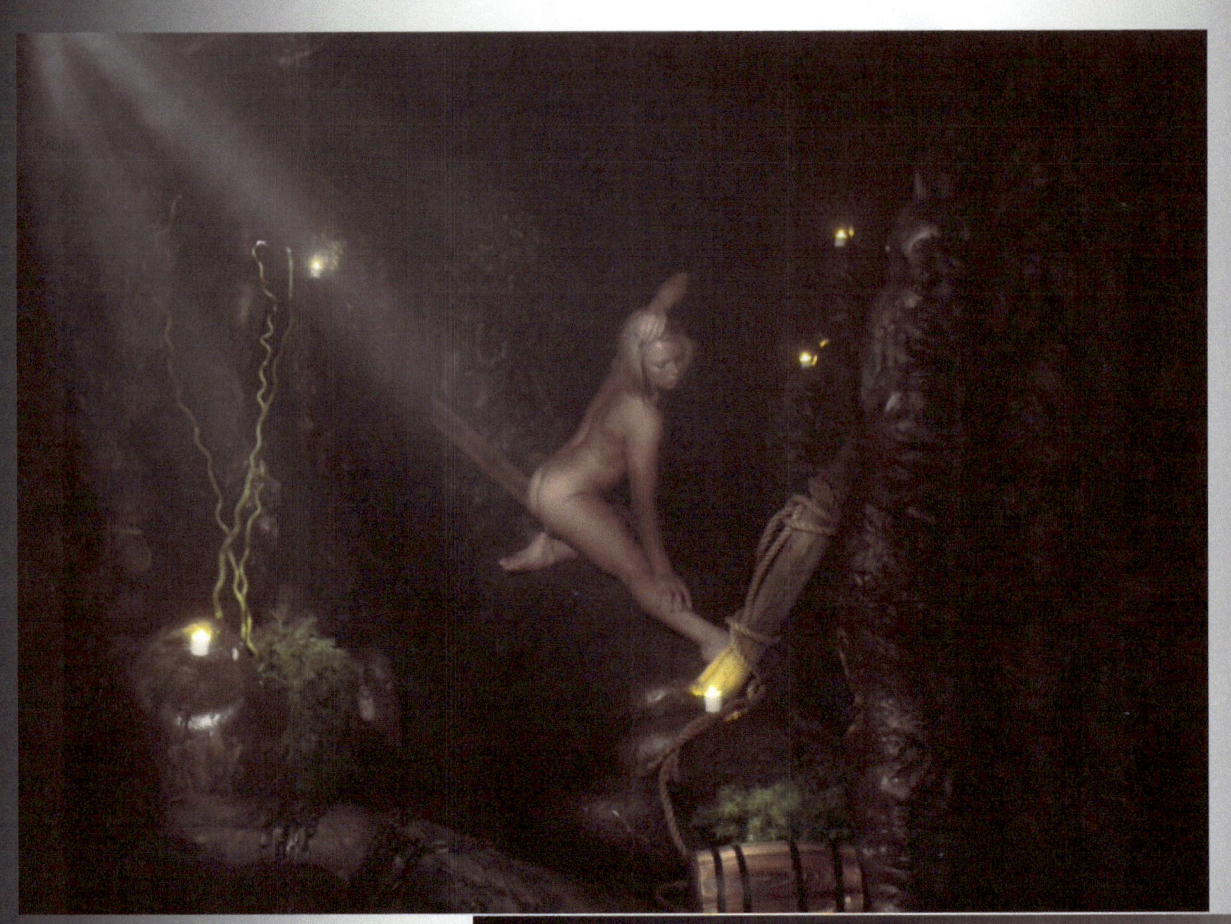

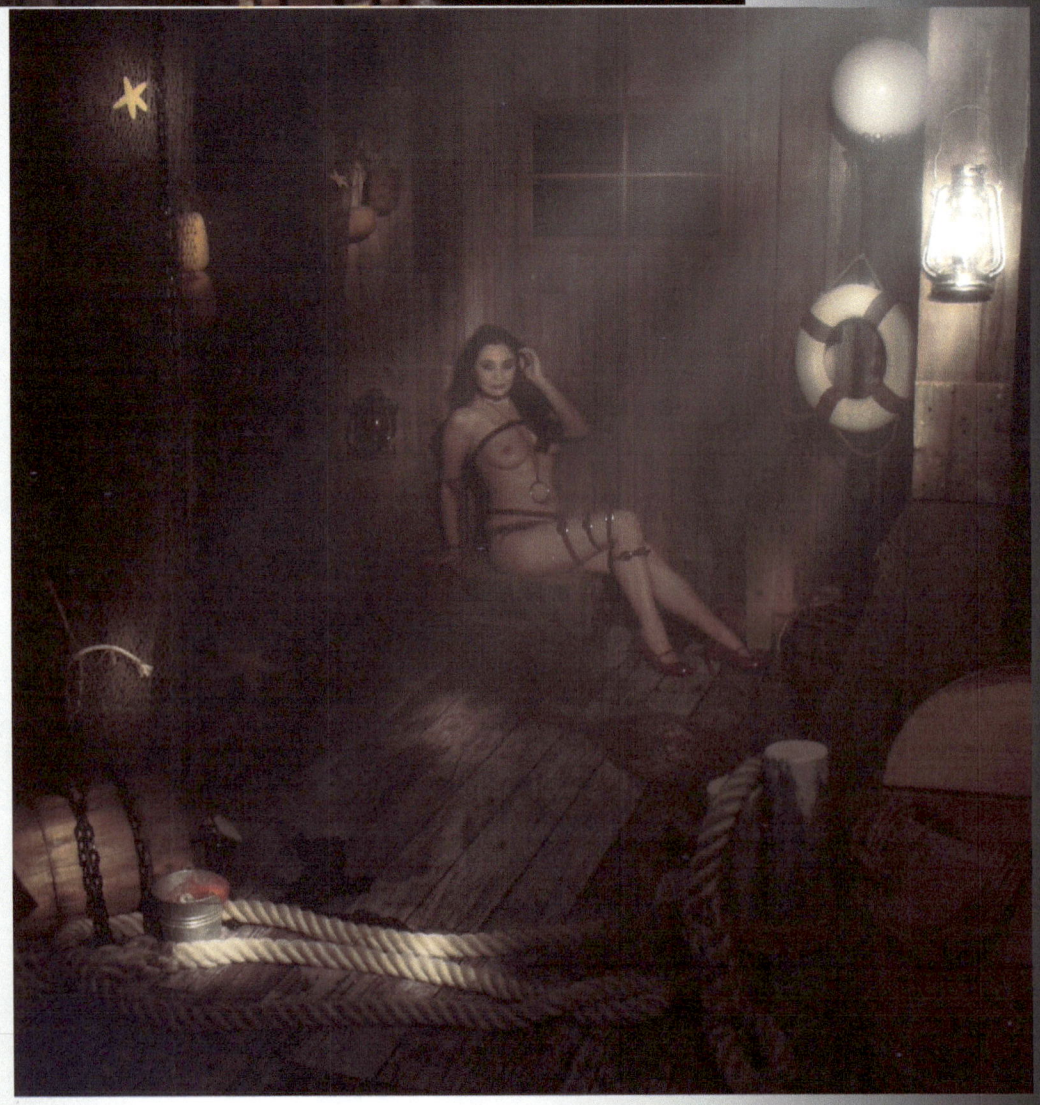

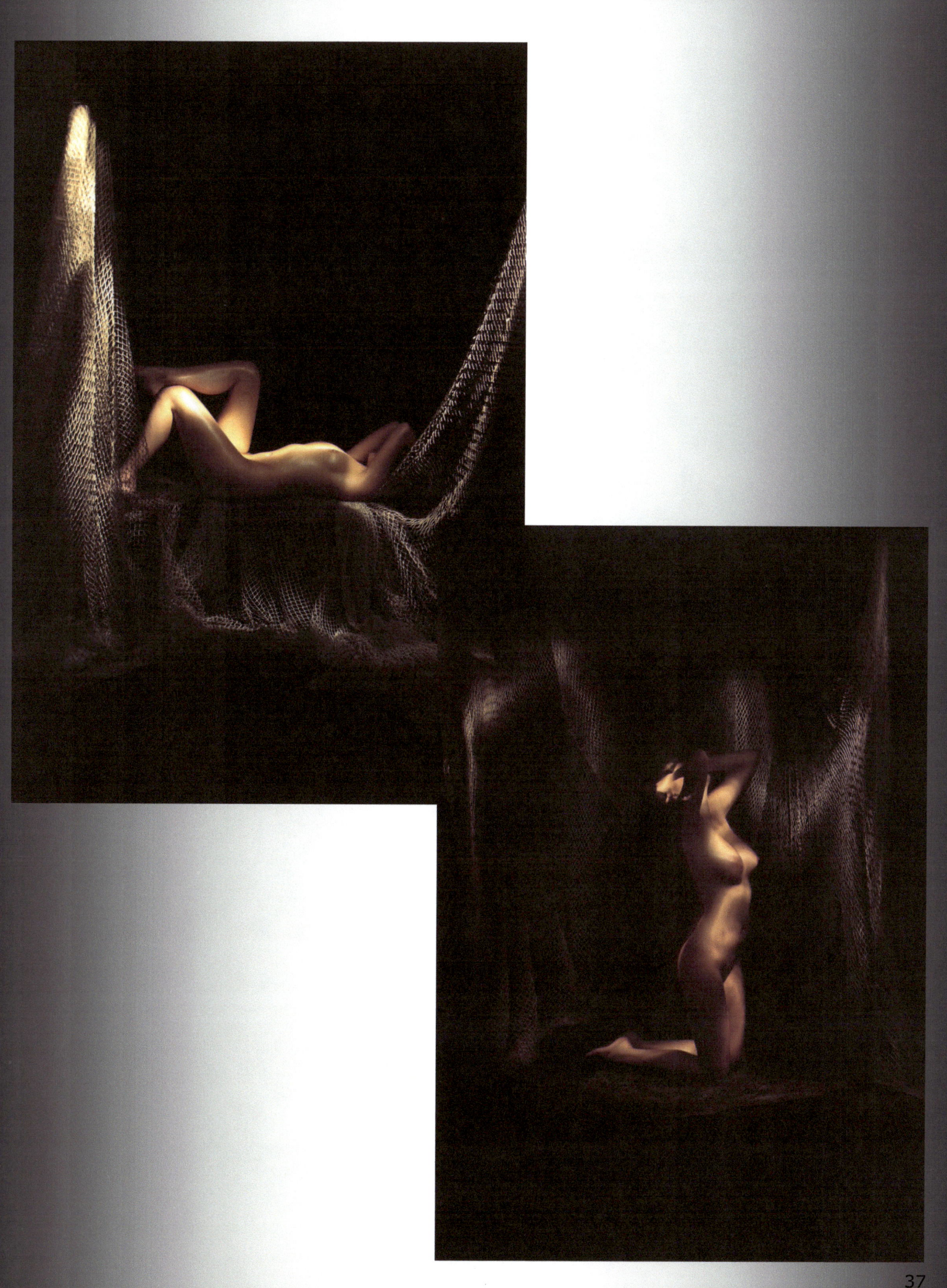

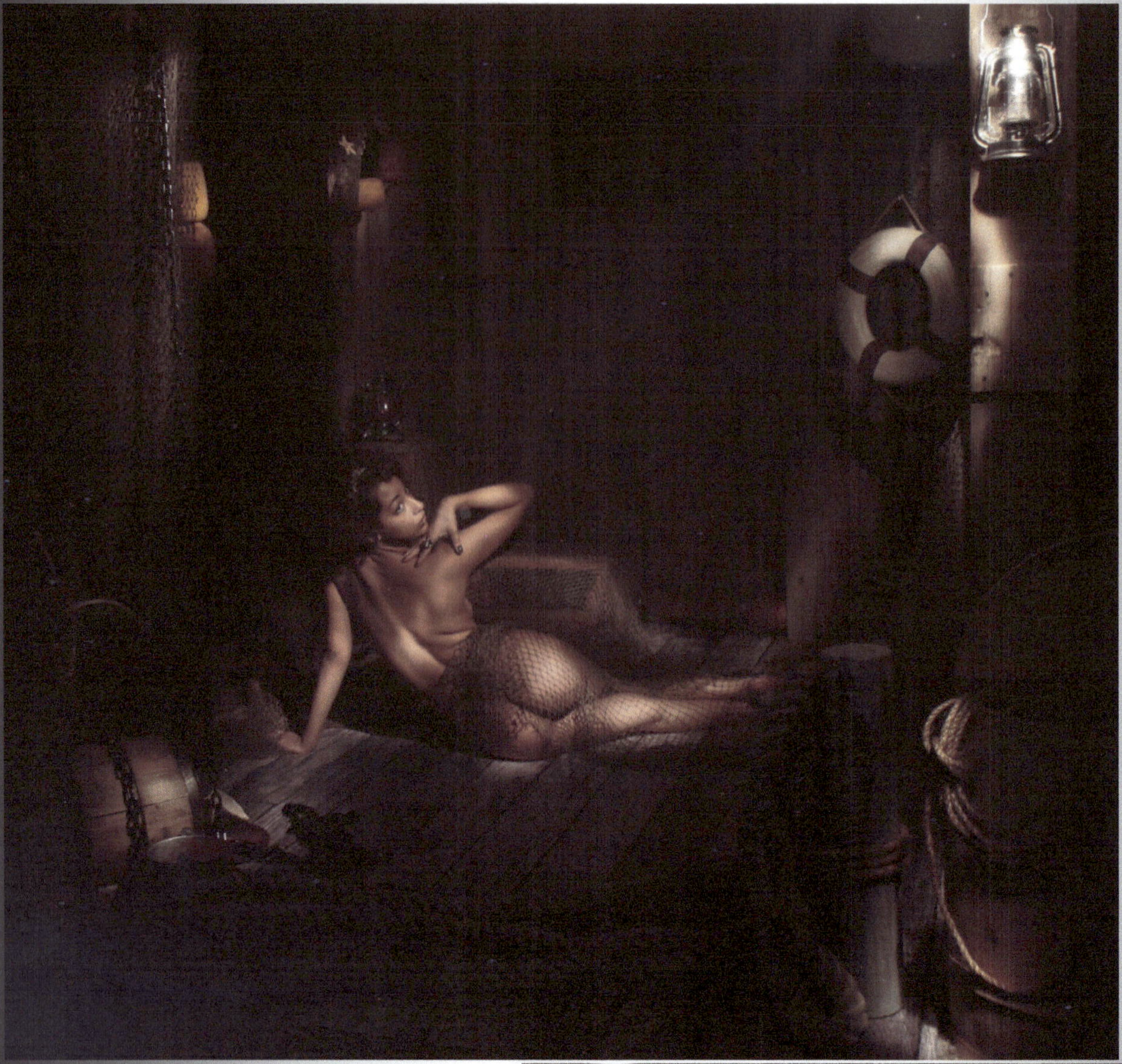

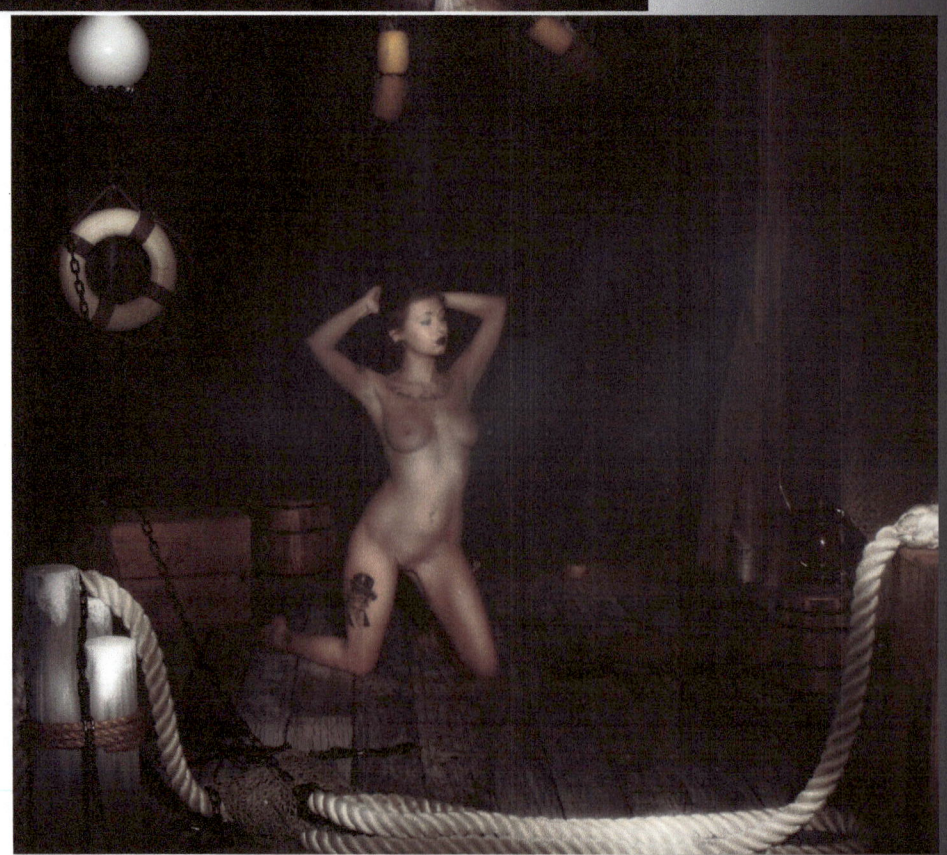

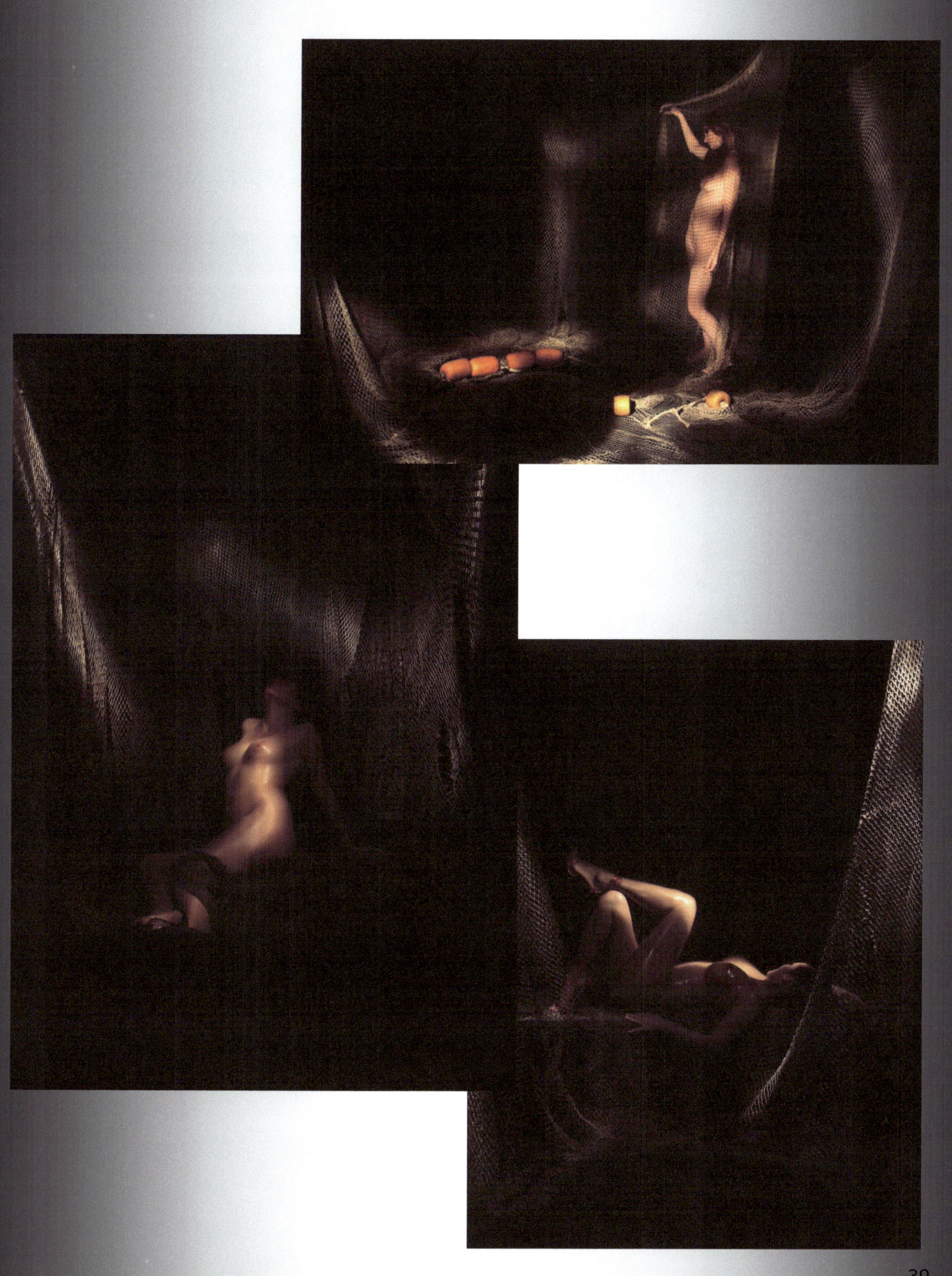

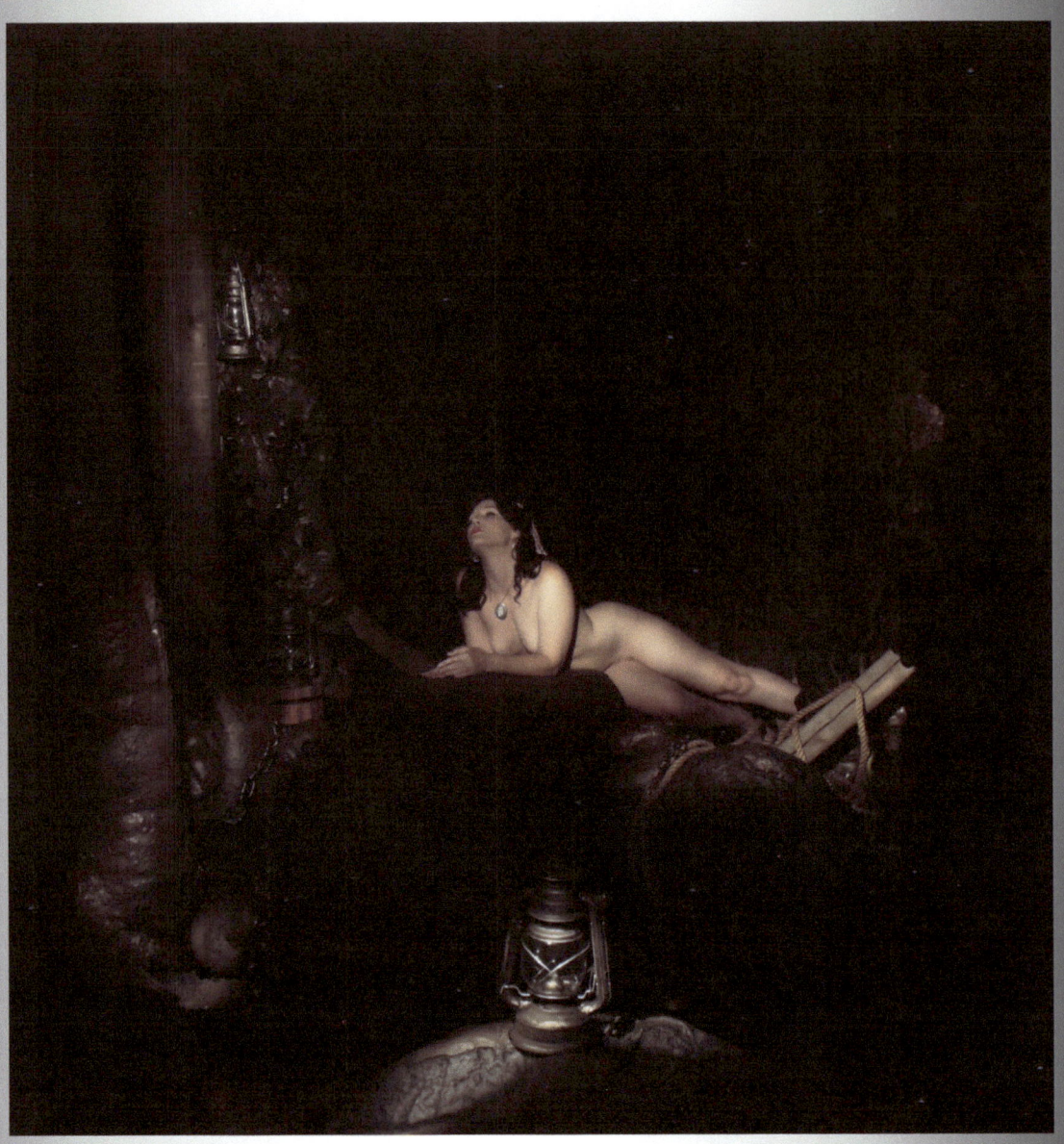

I am photographer Robert Tavernier. My interest in photography began during my time in the Navy, sailing the seas for 21 years. My love of pretty things has developed into a passion for capturing them in images. My interest in artistic nudes comes from an appreciation for how controlling the mood, the look, the lighting, shadows and colors of images can express the real beauty of the human form. Although I have had no formal schooling or training in photography, years of experience with improvisation and simple lighting techniques have helped me to produce the images I love to create and share. I am thankful to my wife Linda for 36 years of support in my endeavors to realize my visions. It all began when she noticed I had taken all of our decorative household plants down into the basement to create my first set. She gave me one week to put her trees back and get my own. Since then I have created my "jungle". And I have built the "dock", where I sit and dream of my old days in the Navy, and the "cave". Honestly, I do have a man cave! I plan to share more of my photographic artwork in future volumes of 'TAVART Nudes"

Contact Robert Tavernier

Www.tavartphotography.com

trobert46@gmail.com

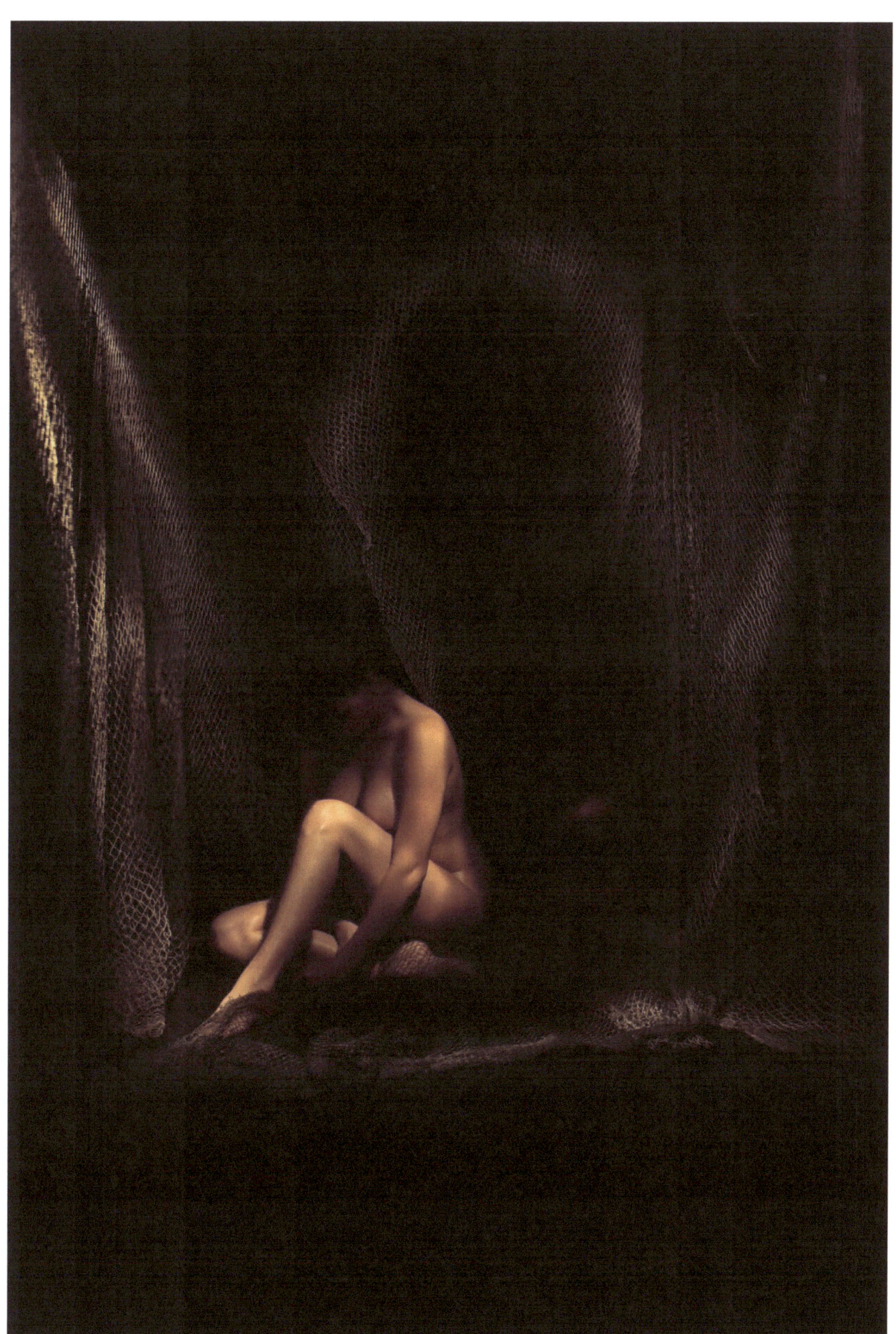

www.ingramcontent.com/pod-product-compliance
Lightning Source LLC
Chambersburg PA
CBHW050838180526
45159CB00004B/1947